HOW CHURCHES GROW

Bernard & Marjorie Palmer

HOW CHURCHES GROW

BETHANY FELLOWSHIP, INC.
Minneapolis, Minnesota

Copyright © 1976
Bethany Fellowship, Inc.
All rights reserved

Published by Bethany Fellowship, Inc.
6820 Auto Club Road, Minneapolis, Minnesota 55438

Printed in the United States of America

Library of Congress Cataloging in Publication Data:

Palmer, Bernard Alvin, 1914-
    How churches grow.

    1. Church growth—Case studies. 2. Evangelistic work—Case
studies. I. Palmer, Marjorie, joint author. II. Title.
BV652.25.P34   254'.5   76-40927
ISBN 0-87123-229-4

BERNARD PALMER is probably America's best-known author of Christian youth books. In addition, he has several adult titles to his credit. He and his wife live in Holdrege, Nebraska. He ia a member of the Board of Publications of the Evangelical Free Church, and is a member of the board of the Tyndale Foundation and Short Terms Abroad.

Preface

Selecting churches for a book of this type is an agonizing process. There are so many that could have been included —so many that probably should have been included, even at the expense of some of those we chose to write about.

Our purpose, as you will see, is not to publicize an individual church or to extol the abilities and virtues of a given pastor. Rather, we hope to show the principles that can make any church effective, regardless of its location, size or financial condition.

One of the congregations we visited made no effort to build up membership. As a result they have 250 on the rolls and an average Sunday morning attendance of 1,000. Another group had a building that would hold less than one-tenth of their current membership at one time. Yet it was adequate. They have only one Sunday morning service. The same method of judging both churches would be grossly inaccurate.

With that in mind we tried to select the base that would more honestly reflect the strength of the work we were writing about.

Bernard and Marjorie Palmer

Contents

1

How It All Began

Starting work on this project we soon discovered that the church is one of the most popular subjects for the writers of religious books today. There are books about the fastest growing congregations [1] and those with the largest Sunday schools. [2] Others extol the gains made by groups relying on the wheels of a fleet of buses and the dedication of drivers and bus captains. [3] Books have been written about congregations stimulated to new effectiveness by the shoe leather of visitation teams using carefully detailed methods, [4] and those that have adopted a radical approach to the problems they see as facing the church today. [5]

Even before we began to visit churches we decided that a narrow definition of the term How Churches Grow would not suit our purpose. The generally accepted meaning refers only to size. The churches we would be considering would have more going for them than a high weekly body count and staggering totals of offerings, buses and square feet of floor space in a sprawling array of buildings.

For the purpose of our evaluation we have broadened the scope of the term to refer to those churches that are growing in effectiveness, regardless of size. We would be interpreting the phrase to include those congregations that are doing an outstanding job of meeting the needs of their people, whether there are 200 or 20,000 on the roles.

Our travels over the next nine months only verified our conclusion that factors other than numbers must be considered. One congregation is struggling against great odds in the heart of a racially mixed inner city. Although the work is often discouraging and growth is marginal when viewed by the standards of less difficult fields, she may actually be achieving more with marginal growth than her flourishing sister in a rapidly expanding middle-class suburb.

There is a church of average size in the Midwest with a long history of establishing 'daughter' congregations and seeing them through the first difficult years to become self-supporting. It would be easy to overlook the effective ministry of such a group because of another, much larger church not far away that draws all her people to a central location.

Evangelism is important, to be sure. It is one of the chief reasons for the existence of the church. Yet we were searching for those churches that made the winning of an individual to Christ the starting point in their ministry, and who presented Jesus Christ as the answer to the problems in the individual's life. In other words, those that minister to the *whole man*, long-time church member and new convert alike. The process of shepherding new believers is slow and time-consuming. It is the same when it comes to helping individuals wrestle with their personal problems. Churches that make a definite effort to help people meet all their needs may be ignored because of the more spectacular growth of those groups who are more superficial in their care of new converts and helping members of their congregation with their problems.

In any given situation we had to examine the type of area in which the church is located and the sort of people the pastor and the congregation are trying to reach. Their financial and educational status makes a difference. So do their denominational backgrounds and their race or nationality.

We have considered all those elements as valid in our search for exploding or growing churches. So in these pages you will find congregations of less than 100 members as well as those of more than 18,000.

We had only two preconceived ideas as we set to work. First: *Size of itself is not an effective measurement of success, nor the lack of it.*

Second: *Program is not necessarily the key to church growth and accomplishment as we are defining them.* While program is important and must be a factor in one's appraisal, the interviews only strengthened our conviction that methods are often greatly overrated.

One church, while conservative in doctrine, we found to be exciting and as modern in methods as tomorrow's newspaper. The pastor and his staff are concerned about evangelism, but they are also concerned about meeting the needs of their people. They are determined to help their constituents to place Christ in every area of their lives. They feel their ministry is with the neighborhood in which their church is located, and use an assortment of unorthodox ways of reaching the people who live nearby.

Another congregation is at the opposite end of the spectrum in everything except doctrine. Conservative to the extreme, their services are at the traditional times of the days of the week and conducted in the traditional manner. It was our considered judgment, based on several hours of interviews, that this congregation had done little that was new and different in the past 25 years.

Both churches, while preaching the same Christ, are as different in methods as they could possibly be. Yet each is meeting the needs of its people and is quite effectively throwing the lifeline of the gospel to the families they are endeavoring to reach.

There are reasons other than program for the success or failure of a church. We had vague, undocumented ideas as to what those reasons were, but we tried to keep from formulating those principles until they began to shout at us from our interviews. It wasn't long in happening. It was then that the project took on new meaning. It blotted out the weariness of crowded airports and the boredom of motels and overpriced cafes.

We were beginning to see the inner workings of God's most important institution on earth—the Christian Church. We were learning why some congregations were successful when others, preaching the same gospel, limped along, year after dismal year. We were understanding the principles behind success— principles ordained by God; principles any pastor, any congregation can use.

Drudgery became an exciting adventure.

Come along with us. Visit the churches we visited. Sit in

the pastors' studies we sat in. Talk with the pastors and laymen we talked with. See for yourself why we have considered these churches *exploding*. Let us show you how it can happen in *your* church.

Notes

1. Elmer Towns, *Great Soul Winning Churches* (Sword of the Lord) and *America's Fastest Growing Churches* (Impact Books). *Great Churches of Today* by staff of *Decision* Magazine (World Wide Publications).
2. Elmer Towns, *The Ten Largest Sunday Schools*.
3. Gardiner Gantry, *Bus Them In* (Church Growth Publications).
4. James Kennedy, *Exploding Evangelism* (Tyndale House).
5. David R. Mains, *Full Circle* (Word).

2

First Mennonite Brethren Church, Wichita, Kansas

It was not coincidence that we began our research with the First Mennonite Brethren Church in Wichita that cold afternoon in early January. God guided us there, although we were scarcely aware of it at the time.

When Rev. Dale Warkentin, five years out of Fuller Theological Seminary, was called to Wichita in 1967, the church was small and quite ineffectual in reaching beyond its own circle. Most of the 140 who worshipped there were of Mennonite background, and there seemed to be little hope of breaking out of that ethnic prison. Their uninformed neighbors looked on them as weird people who scorned cars and electricity and refused to educate their children. They avoided them as though even casual association would somehow be contaminating.

Today those walls are broken down. Attendance averages close to 300, with most of the growth coming among couples with small children and the newly married. Many are new believers, brought to a saving knowledge of Jesus Christ by exuberant young men and women who knew nothing about Him themselves until a year or so before.

The pastor was astonished when he saw the results of a survey the congregation completed in 1972. It revealed that there were at least 20 men and women who had been reached for Christ by people in the church whom he had not even heard about.

But those things did not happen magically, nor did they come about by reason of some simple, easy formula. The roots went back to his days at seminary.

"I was at Fuller when Dr. Virgil Gerber and his staff were working out the techniques for measuring and evaluating evangelism and church growth," the youthful pastor told us. "That was before he had finished the manual that came out of those studies.[1] I had been deeply impressed by the philosophy of using scientific methods for measuring what is happening in the local church, and I had access to much of Dr. Gerber's material.

"I also was aware of the PERT[2] method of evaluating the strengths and weaknesses of various departments in industrial plants and has now been adapted for use in the local church.[3]"

The church adaptation weighs what is being done in each department—the Sunday school, youth work, women's department, missionary society, choir, and every other area of the ministry.

Selling the board on the project was not too difficult, but getting the individual in the pew to understand the purpose of the program and to get behind it presented certain problems.

"We'd be doing a lot more for the Lord if we spent that time in visitation," one of the older men complained.

"You're not getting me to fill out any questionaire," another retorted bluntly. "It's nobody's business what I know or don't know about the Bible, or when I last talked to anybody about Jesus Christ."

Resisting the natural impulse of youth to press for an immediate decision, Warkentin presented the program in detail from the pulpit and in visiting with those he knew to have reservations about it. It wasn't long until he discovered that the underlying reason behind most of the opposition was the fear that the raw material on filled-out questionaires would reveal their identity. The forms weren't to be signed. However, some thought that the pastor would learn who they were by noting their handwriting.

"We got around this by feeding the material into one of the many computers available to us around the city," Rev. Warkentin informed us. "The computer was not necessary to the success of the survey, but when the people realized I wasn't even going to see the handwritten questionaires they were more at ease.

"Those questionaires were a revelation to me," he told us.

"I discovered that I had been taking far too much for granted in my assumption of what our people knew about the Bible. To be sure, we had quite a number of new believers in our congregation and those who were interested but had never personally received Christ. Still, I have to confess that I was shocked at some of the answers.

"We had people who didn't believe that man is a sinner and needs saving. Others didn't know the answers to some of the most elementary biblical questions. I had erred drastically in assuming they all had reached a given level of understanding."

As a result of that survey he went back to preaching a certain number of sermons each month on the most elementary Bible truths.

"I discovered that I couldn't assume our people knew anything about the Word of God." And, as though afraid we might misunderstand, he went on quietly. "I don't believe our people have any less knowledge than the average congregation. There has always been sound Bible teaching from this pulpit. I think the difference is that we *know* they don't understand."

When the survey was completed and the evaluation finished, the church leaders met for a weekend. They went over the results carefully so they could understand the strengths and weaknesses of each department of the church. They agreed on goals and in most cases how to implement them. This is done now on a yearly basis. The progress in each area of activity is carefully plotted.

One of the first problems the young pastor wrestled with was that of improving the image of the church.

"We Mennonites may have more difficulties in this area than others," he said, "because of the confusion in peoples' minds between those of us who live normally and the fringe groups like the Amish who have customs that make them stand out. Basically, however, I think most evangelicals are thought of as fanatics by the world. So, I'm sure this is a problem we all face."

A Social Concerns Committee was set up and charged with the responsibility of showing Christian love and interest to individuals and families in time of sorrow or need. When there is a sudden death in the northwest section of Wichita, a card, together with a letter of sympathy, is sent from the church office. If anyone in the congregation knows the deceased or is acquainted with some member of the family, he sends some food.

"It's surprising what a meat loaf or a baked dish will do at a time like that," Rev. Warkentin said. "I don't know how many times I've had folks phone me to thank me for our little expression of thoughtfulness. One man said, 'I didn't know the church was aware that we existed.'

"Of course I have to continually preach about Christ's compassion and our Christian responsibilities toward those around us. Nothing would be more empty than going through the motions of being concerned in order to gain favor with such people."

The Mennonites have long been active in humanitarian causes and the Wichita church, although most of the growth is being drawn from the outside, assumes its share of social activity. The people take part in the Mennonite Disaster Service, an inter-Mennonite project, and assume responsibility for helping provide funds and manpower.

This, too, has helped to break down the barriers against them.

"I want to make it plain," the pastor said, "that whatever we do in this area is an expression of Christian love and concern. It is not a substitute for the gospel of Christ."

When the flood devastated Rapid City, South Dakota, in 1972, volunteers from the Wichita church took time off from their work and went to help with the clean up.

"We didn't alert the news people or make any attempt to get publicity," Rev. Warkentin told us, "but the story got out. We were given excellent coverage by the local TV, radio and newspaper reporters."

When a tornado struck a farming area a few miles from Wichita, the church sent a crew to help clean away the wrecked buildings and put things in order again. When a river flooded they had a group of men filling sandbags and stacking them in place to protect homes and property.

As a result of the survey and evaluation the morning worship service was changed to one less formal, a committee on outreach was set up, the youth program was sharpened, and other changes were made in established areas of the ministry.

"Occasionally there is a dialogue on Sunday morning in

addition to the sermon," the pastor explained, "and we use different methods to open the morning service."

The Christmas just prior to our visit one of the men took a large package with him to the platform for the invocation. He talked at length about the beautiful wrapping, showing them it had a different kind of paper and ribbons on each side. Then he went back and sat down. Somebody from the congregation asked him if he wasn't going to open it and see what was inside.

He looked surprised.

"Oh? Is there something inside?"

This was the introduction to the pastor's message on the true meaning of Christmas.

On occasion kids in sneakers and blue jeans, like the Hallelujah Joy Band that appeared recently, have taken over the entire morning service with their guitars and drums and amplifiers. The next Sunday the congregation will sing "Just as I Am" the way they have always done.

"I've had to be careful to prepare our older people for the change in the service," Warkentin told us. "I know a good many of them don't particularly enjoy the kids' type of music, but most of them are glad to see us use it because they know it is a way of getting and holding the kids."

"I wouldn't go to *any other* church," one fuzzy cheeked member of the anti-establishment people announced firmly after his conversion to Jesus Christ a few weeks before. "As a matter of fact, I'm really against the church."

When asked why he came to services if he felt that way, his expression changed, but he saw nothing incongruous about his position. "I come because things are different here."

That difference could be summed up in one word—*love*.

Young couples who were unbelievers themselves two or three years earlier are reaching out to touch the troubled lives around them. Bartenders and barmaids whose lives have been a tangled mass of marriages, broken homes and remarriages, torn by drunkenness and infidelity, have received Jesus Christ. They are so remarkably transformed that their former friends look in awe at them.

One young man became a Christian as a result of the Campus Crusade survey conducted by the youth of the church. They knocked on his door at a critical time. He and his wife were having serious problems, and it looked as though their marriage was headed for divorce.

He didn't give the visitors any indication of interest. Quite the opposite. He wasn't even respectful enough to stay his profanity. His answers indicated he knew little about Christ.

But he was interested and he and his wife decided to visit the church. He didn't know its name but she remembered from having seen it on some of the material they were using. The couple began to attend the Sunday morning service. It wasn't long until he received Christ and was baptized.

One Sunday not long after that, he got to his feet an instant before the pastor gave the invocation and announced that he would like to say something. That sort of thing happens occasionally.

"You folks all know about the change that has come into my life. I want to tell you how happy I am to be a Christian and to have our home restored and peaceful. I know it was because an awful lot of you were praying for me—for us. I want to thank you for it."

One couple who lived near the church watched in amazement as the parking lot filled Sunday after Sunday and the morning service was crowded out. Although they themselves wouldn't attend, they urged some of their relatives to start.

The young man and his new wife were having a difficult struggle, and the family that lived near the church was con-concerned about them. They knew the kids wanted to clean up their lives, but didn't have the determination or the will power for it. The wife had been on drugs and they were having marital difficulties. There seemed to be no hope for them.

"You should go to church," their relatives told them. "Maybe that would help."

"No way." The young man was adamant. "We've already tried the church." He named a nearby group that was a part of a liberal demonination. "We were there three or four times, but it didn't have anything for either of us."

They objected strenuously at first, thinking they were being asked to attend a sect that refused to recognize the arrival of the 20th century. When they were assured that a lot of couples their age attended, they decided to try it but only for one Sunday.

Today they are there every Sunday. They have learned that Christ can do for them what they could not do for themselves.

He has been able to clean up their lives and to make their home respectable and harmonious. Now they have a beautiful baby and, for the first time in their lives, know what true happiness is.

"God could have done all kinds of things to me because of the way I've lived," the wife confided to the pastor, referring to the effect of drugs on the children of drug addicts. "But He didn't. He gave me a healthy baby. How we praise Him for it."

The survey and evaluation program revealed a need for more fellowship among those who attend the church. "I doubt that we would even have been aware of it otherwise, but our questionaire revealed that it was lacking," the pastor related. "We could have encouraged our people to visit among themselves on an informal basis, but we wanted the program to be a part of the ministry of the church. We felt that it could be another form of outreach."

For that reason Friendship groups involving the entire congregation have been organized. There are 15 or 20 small units which are asked to meet once a month. The format is loose and simple and varies to some extent from one group to another. They meet in one of the homes or a cafe and for a program have a short devotional or a list of questions for the master of ceremonies to use to spark a sharing session.

The loosely organized Friendship clubs, which have been meeting for more than three years, used to shuffle their membership every three months to avoid the danger of building cliques within the church. Now the reshuffling occurs every six months.

On one occasion they divided the people by occupations or professions as much as possible. All the teachers, medical people, contractors, and so on, were placed in the same groups. It gave the men an opportunity to discuss the specific ethical problems facing them. The groups have been divided by streets and neighborhoods, alphabetically and any number of other ways.

"It's amazing how those groups have forged a bond of love between us," one of the laymen said.

The principles of small groups is not limited to the Friendship clubs, whose chief purpose is Christian fellowship. The church also has a number of Discovery groups that meet for the purpose of discussing Christian ethics and separation and the application of biblical principles to the lives of individuals.

"Our survey showed a need in this area," the pastor explained. "We have always thought of ourselves as a Bible-teaching church, and in one way we have been. But, far too many of our people were drawing a hard line between their secular lives and their spiritual lives. The Discovery groups have helped us to erase that distinction and to apply the teachings of God to every area of our lives."

The same practical aspects of the Discovery groups have spilled over into certain classes of the Sunday school. Because of the response to those small group meetings, a class on business ethics was taught in Sunday school by a dedicated young accountant. One individual, whose occupation will remain secret, was visibly touched by the series of lessons. He had been in the church only a year and was new at the whole business of a personal relationship with Jesus Christ. He was a believer but had never understood how Christian ethics and morality relate to one's everyday life.

"I've never been exposed to anything like this," he confided to the pastor.

Another young man, 25 or 26 years old, was earning a fantastic salary. However, he was in a position where he had to pay off people in order to get business. What he was doing wasn't illegal, but it skirted the outer limits of the law and ethically was in the same category as paying a politician for a contract to build a bridge. Because he was convicted of it as a believer, he quit the job and turned down an offer of a similar nature where he would have been required to do much the same thing.

Another man served notice on his boss that he was quitting his job because he had been ordered to lie to customers. Still another was making a change because he and the other salesmen for the company were forced to sell computers that did not exist.

"It's this sort of devotion to Jesus Christ that attracts those outside the church," the pastor told us.

The principle of small Bible clubs has been effective in helping the church to work with the high school gang. Most of the clubs meet in the schools. The Lord has given them a number of talented, popular kids, which has encouraged others to align themselves with Jesus Christ. The quarterback of the Northwest Wichita High School football team calls the Mennonite Brethren Church his church home. So do two of the cheer leaders and a popular teenaged disc jockey on a local radio station.

As we pried deeper into the inner workings of the local church, we discovered that there were many, perhaps a majority, in the congregation who had a deep commitment to Christ.

It revealed itself in many ways. One fellow recommended the church to a research chemist because he saw that commitment in the lives of the pastor and some members of the congregation.

He was playing poker at the home of a friend, but his mind wasn't on the game. He drew a card almost absentmindedly and turned to the player on his left.

"You've got to be kidding," he exploded. "I don't have a horse and buggy and I'm sure not going to put a little doily on my wife's head and run around every Sunday in a black suit and funny hat."

"I'm serious. We go there once in awhile ourselves. It's not all that bad. The fact is, you might like it."

The following Sunday morning he was in church with his wife, and a few days later Rev. Warkentin went to call on them. The chemist was as blunt with the pastor as he had been with his friend.

"I'd just as well tell you right now that I've never gone to church. I don't know if there is a God and I don't have any need for Him if there is. I'm quite capable of taking care of myself.

"If you want the truth, that wife of mine is a religious fanatic and is about to drive me up the wall. I finally decided I wasn't going to have this continual hassle in our marriage. The other night I told her that I'd go to church with her for six weeks. Then I'll make up my mind whether or not to keep going."

He didn't receive Christ during those six weeks. His resentments and hostility were too deeply rooted for such a sudden transformation, but his agnosticism was gone. He now accepted the fact that there is a God. There was something about the preaching and the sincerity of the congregation that got hold of him. And, besides, somebody asked him to play on the church basketball team. So he kept coming. In less than a year he confessed his sin and asked Jesus Christ to save him and give him a new life.

The preaching of the Word and the association with dedicated believers who lived their faith succeeded where his wife's continual talking only antagonized.

"Of course," Pastor Warkentin remarked, "she was the one who got him to come to church in the first place."

The church does not have a full-fledged recreation program, but the basketball team that interested the research chemist was organized by the former pastor. It is in the Wichita Church League and has been an effective means of outreach among the younger adults.

We were told about a young professional man who recently made a decision for Christ because he liked to play basketball.

He started coming because he wanted Bible training for his family, but our informant did not think he would have kept coming if it hadn't been for basketball.

"He'd played in high school and college, and the opportunity to play again kept him interested until he responded to the gospel and received Christ as his Saviour."

Actually, the basketball team is one more avenue that develops the bond of love and fellowship within the congregation. Most of the wives are interested and follow the team. Some very rewarding friendships have developed which have helped them spiritually.

"I know we aren't exploiting every possibility of using the team as a means of outreach," the pastor went on, thinking over the program soberly. "But one of our long-range goals is to make every avenue of the church a means of deepening the spiritual commitment of the believers and reaching out to the world. If a program fails to meet that standard, it should be dropped, and it will be . . ."

As we finished the interviews at Wichita's First Mennonite Brethren Church and moved to our next stop, we considered all that we had been told.

"What do you think is the most significant factor in that church's success?" I asked Marge.

She thought for a moment. "Well, it all seemed to begin to move forward when they took a good look at themselves and decided where they were strong and where they were weak."

I couldn't help smiling. We had both reached the same conclusion. I opened my notebook and handed it to her. At the top of the page I had written, "There is one lesson to be drawn from the First Mennonite Brethren Church in Wichita, Kansas. If you would have an effective local congregation, there is a 'best' place to start: ANALYZE AND EVALUATE.

The more we thought about it the more convinced we were that our appraisal was correct, but we weren't ready to speak of it yet. Before stating them to be true, we had determined to verify each principle for church growth in other churches as well.

Notes

1. Virgil Gerber, *Manual for Evangelism/Church Growth* (William Carey Library).

2. *Program Evaluation in Review Technique* (developed by Robert McNamara, former Secretary of Defense when he was in industry).

3. *Evaluation Review Technique* (prepared by MARC, 919 W. Huntington Drive, Monrovia, California 91016).

Faith Baptist Church, Fort Wayne, Indiana

As I slipped a cassette into the recorder and opened my notebook once more, three words shouted at me from the top of the page: ANALYZE AND EVALUATE!

I wondered whether we would find that to be as true here as it had been in Wichita.

The situation was somewhat different in that Rev. Joseph Baker had moved to Fort Wayne in the fall of 1967 for the purpose of organizing a new congregation.

"I had more than seventeen years of experience in the pastorate at that time," he began, "the promise of a sizable subsidy from the American Baptist Convention, and some new principles I was anxious to try."

While he had made no formal measurment of the work being done by the various departments in his former churches, his experience had sparked the development of certain ideas. A new church without a background of tradition was an ideal place to initiate new methods.

We soon discovered that Rev. Baker's philosophy of an effective church was similar to that of the Wichita pastor. He, too, had been analyzing and evaluating, although from years of experience and not a formal survey. He was basing his conclusions on what had been done in his previous charges, but was making changes as the new work was organized. Rev. Warkentin and his board worked within the church they surveyed and evaluated. Today Rev. Baker's principles have also been proven sound. Faith Baptist Church has an active congregation of 580, with 46 new families added to their number in 1973. The increase is still continuing with an average of 20 or more visitors every Sunday. In 1968 the church had a subsidy of $12,000 from the denomination. The amount was cut in half in 1969 and to $1,900 in 1970, the final year of outside financial assistance. In 1973 the total contributions were more than $83,000 and they were aiming for $100,000 in 1974.

Faith Baptist Church has been founded and solidly established through the use of small Inquiry and Faith-Action groups, which are basically Bible studies. There is a special emphasis on winning and recruiting men.

"For years I've been concerned about the scarcity of men in the average congregation," Rev. Baker informed us as we sat across the desk from him in the study of the church building that is already too small. "I was sure God had revealed the reason for this to me a few months before in my Kansas City pastorate and I thought I knew how to overcome it. Fort Wayne would give me the opportunity to find out."

Not that he wanted to make the move. He had always pastored an established church and was inexperienced in the special problems of organizing a new work. Moreover, he had never considered himself psychologically, emotionally, or spiritually equipped to go into a new area, however needy, and organize a congregation. That was a task that called for a different personality and different talents than he had.

It seemed to him that the denomination had always sent young, inexperienced men, or those who had difficulty in the places they were serving, to do the church planting. The results had, for the most part, been so disappointing they decided to try a mature, experienced minister who had been reasonably successful in the past.

Rev. Baker was their choice.

However, he was less than eager. The first time they contacted him he turned them down flatly and hoped that would be the end of it. Five months later they approached him again. With some reluctance he agreed to look over the field. When he returned to Kansas City, he had decided on accepting the challenge Fort Wayne presented.

"I had to change my entire frame of reference," he told us. "In previous churches much of my thinking had been in terms of program and providing adequate facilities for carrying it out. Here in Fort Wayne in the fall of 1967 neither program nor a building meant a thing at the moment. Our first concern was for people. We didn't have any. We didn't even have a nucleus."

And there was only one way he knew to get people. Go out and start knocking on doors. He and his family arrived in the Indiana city on October 12 and the evening of the 13th he made his first call.

He subscribed to the Credit Bureau Bulletin which listed the new arrivals and continued his visitation. The response to those early efforts was about the same as he and his people find today. An average of ten or eleven calls were made before he found one couple who was interested enough to attend an Inquiry group.

They were warm and friendly enough to be encouraging and were apologetic as they admitted they weren't attending services anywhere. Still, they were evasive when he tried to find a night when they were free. One or the other had something to do on Monday, Tuesday and Wednesday evenings. When he finally learned they were not committed for Thursday, he asked if he could use their home that night. They eyed each other.

"What are you going to do?" the man asked Baker.

"I'm going to find four or five other couples who are interested and we're going to explore the Christian faith together. We'll be studying the Bible," he explained.

The man was interested. "I've always wanted to know more about the Bible."

"We don't call our groups Bible studies, but that's actually what they are. We've found a great deal of interest in the Word of God among those outside the church."

The wife didn't mind the idea of the couples coming into her home on Thursday night, but she wasn't sure she wanted to fix lunch for them. When she learned she had only to make a pot of coffee and come up with a few cookies she agreed.

On October 29 they had their first meeting and were so well received that an Inquiry group was formed. The first spade of dirt for the new congregation was turned. Today Baker has had 72 such groups, each meeting for six weeks. Using the Bible as the only text the group discussed the question, "What is the mission of the church and Jesus Christ for our time?" In the second meeting they considered the content of the Christian faith as it relates to the symbols in the sanctuary.

"I started the second meeting with a study on the congregation as a symbol of the people of God," Rev. Baker went on. "Actually, we could find nothing that exactly fitted our needs, so I developed my own course of study."

Then he moved to the cross. Since there were a number present from more formal groups, he also dealt with the crucifix, pointing to the differences in the basic beliefs of the Baptist and liturgical churches. From there, he went to the baptistry, the open Bible, the candlesticks, and other symbols.

"I realize there are some dangers in a course like this," he explained, "Such topics can become philosophical or even argumentative and divisive if the leader doesn't exercise great care. But, handled properly, they are an excellent vehicle for considering what the Bible has to say about the essentials of our faith in Jesus Christ. This is what we endeavor to do."

The first inquiry group was just getting under way when the second was organized. By the end of the year there were 5 with a total of 32 couples. When all 5 had finished their series of meetings, there were enough people interested to provide a nucleus for starting services. Still, he wasn't ready. There was much more to be done.

The last of November, Baker and his wife started the Sunday school with 18 persons other than the 5 members of their family.

Pastor Baker had first seen the value of small group Bible studies when he was pastoring in Kansas City, and one of his members asked him if he could help her to be more bold in sharing Jesus Christ with others.

"I was disturbed as I went over the various church activities and realized there was nothing in the program to meet her need," he told us. "This ought to be a basic area of concern in the church of Christ, and we were doing absolutely nothing to prepare our people for it."

That was when the first Faith-Action groups began. They were somewhat different than the Inquiry groups in that they were developed for believers to help them understand the Word of God and how they can relate their faith to their everyday lives.

As the pastor talked I looked at Marge. The Mennonite church in Wichita had the same sort of Bible studies for believers, only they went by a different name.

Rev. Baker made no claim to originating the principle (and neither did Rev. Warkentin). Such Bible study cells have been around for years with varying degrees of success. The Baptist pastor was first introduced to the method by Roger Fredrickson, pastor of the First Baptist Church in Sioux Falls, South Dakota, who has approximately 80 such groups operating at one time in his church. Applying the idea to church planting, however, is Baker's own.

Early in our interview he mentioned his concern that so few men were involved in many churches around the country.

"I had never understood why that was true until I called on a home in Kansas City," he said. "When I stopped at the house in the afternoon and found the family gone I made my next visit to that home at night.

"It was purely a visit of convenience. They lived some distance from us and I didn't want to take the time for a special trip the next day."

"I'm sure glad a preacher has finally gotten around to calling on us," the husband said.

His wife scolded him, reminding him that the minister of the church they used to attend had called on them a number of times.

"Maybe he did," the man retorted, testily, "but I never got to see him. He didn't come when I was around."

That harsh indictment smote Baker. What the man said was true.

"It was as though somebody had suddenly drawn a curtain back so I could see the situation as it appeared to my host. My formal calls shouted to the man that the church and the minister weren't interested in him. All that mattered was his wife and kids.

"I realized, then, that we had few men in so many churches because we were taking the easy road, as pastors, by doing our visitation at a time that is convenient for us, and not when the men were home.

"I tried calling at night in Kansas City and found my efforts somewhat more successful than in the past, but it was not until we started working in Fort Wayne that we realized the full potential of evening calls as it relates to reaching men."

Out of 190 families who have been involved in the church

since the beginning, 175 have included the men. (Thirty families have moved away since 1968, leaving a net gain of 160 families.)

The Inquiry groups were highly successful in supplying the nucleus for the new church—far more successful than even Baker had anticipated they would be. And, surprisingly, he had few changes or adaptations to make, save for a few groups of couples with small children. They suggested the study sessions be lengthened to cover more material so they could be concluded in four weeks rather than six. It meant saving the services of a baby sitter for two evenings.

By the end of 1968 there were 74 family units on the church rolls with a total membership of 190 and an active resident constituency of 296. Most of those members came into the church by means of the Inquiry groups.

But to Pastor Baker the visitation seemed endless.

"I don't really like the conclusions I've reached regarding visitation," he told us. "But they are based on our experience and I'm convinced that they're true. My personal inclination has always been to reserve my evenings for myself and my family. Our early efforts at Fort Wayne, however, showed us that if I wanted to get the church off the ground I had to continue calling at night."

There is a direct relationship between the number of calls made in a month and the gain in people, his records show. Although he usually makes far more calls than he suggests to other pastors, he is convinced that 100 visits per month are an absolute minimum.

"And to be effective with me," he added, "the bulk of those calls have to be made at night."

o   o   o

As Dorothea and Richard Walls related their experience, we saw again that love for both God and man are absolute essentials for a thriving church. They are 34 and 36 years old, respectively, and have three children ranging in ages from 5 to 15. They were Christians from another denomination but their dedication to Christ was marred by indifference. They were looking for a church home after moving to Fort Wayne two months before, and decided to go to the Faith Baptist

Church because it was conveniently close to their home.

"Rev. Baker made five or six calls on us in a two-week period," Mrs. Walls told us. "He was so warm and friendly we quit looking elsewhere for a church and visited an Inquiry group."

Indifference kept their attendance spotty for several months. Then their oldest son was seriously injured and had to have his spleen removed. They were just far enough removed from the church in their own thinking that they did not contact the pastor, but Rev. Baker contacted them. He was at the hospital twice a day as long as Jeff Walls was there.

"Neither my husband nor I were there when he came, but Jeff would tell us about his visits," Mrs. Walls said. " 'That preacher was here again,' he would say. 'He even knows my name!'

"He made Jeff feel that he was important and showed him that he was honestly concerned about him."

When the 15-year-old boy was released from the hospital, Rev. Baker continued to call on him. It made a lasting impression on all the family.

"But it wasn't only the friendliness of the pastor that attracted us to Faith Baptist Church," Mr. Walls put in. "It's the friendliness of the members, too. They're just like Baker. They're concerned about each other and the rest of us they get acquainted with. When Jeff was hurt they were all praying for him and calling to see how he was doing." He paused. "And you want to know something. They've been so concerned for us we've learned to love and be concerned about them too. We really *care* about people now." He paused. "It's strange how that works."

As Rev. Baker continued his door-to-door visitation, he came to see the image most others have of the average Baptist church.

"It wasn't good," he told us. "So many were turned off by what they thought we were—judging us for what they believed us to be. Now I don't care what the world thinks of us unless it causes them to close their ears to the gospel of Jesus Christ, but that was what was happening."

He began to ask some of those who were cold and unresponsive what they thought of when he said 'Baptist.'

"You're the ones who picketed the courthouse in Indianapolis when Kennedy ran for president," one woman said. "You thought the Pope was going to take over the country."

"You won't let your people do anything," someone else told him.

Rev. Baker realized, then, that most of the people outside Christian circles thought they knew what his church was against but had no idea what it was for.

"We were going to have to change our image if we were to reach those we were burdened for," he told us. "We preach salvation by grace but leave the impression of salvation by keeping our laws."

When their constitution was drawn up the church did not, specifically, name the sins to be avoided.

"I preach living a dedicated life and allowing our love for Christ to guide us in all areas of our lives. Those principles are also an important part of the teaching of our Faith-Action groups. We want to challenge our congregation to live separated lives because of their own convictions and their deep love for God, not because we have set down some rules."

The method seems to be working. Families who might otherwise have refused to come to the church at all are coming and finding Christ as Saviour. And, as they grow in their faith, many are voluntarily accepting the standards they abhorred before.

"The thing that first appealed to my wife and me about this church," one of the men shared with us, "was the preaching of Christ and how relating Him to today's problems can help us in our daily walk. . . . I still forget occasionally that God has made my business what it is and I want to run it my way. I'm conscious of sin now, and some of the sins I still commit. But the strong emphasis on the teachings of Christ from the pulpit and in the groups have helped me to remember that my old self gets in the way. I've been able to rectify those things and clean up my life. It's slow, but I feel I'm growing spiritually."

The same concern about the needs of people has caused the church to organize a special Bible study for divorced men and women. The attendance only averages six or seven but it fills a very real need.

"Those who are divorced," Rev. Baker said, "and especially the women, have all the emotional and financial problems of the average widow, plus feelings of guilt and inferiority and rejection few outsiders can understand.

"She is drained emotionally by the ordeal she has just been through. If she has small children, and most of them do, there are the usual financial difficulties of taking care of their physical needs, and the problem of providing discipline and a stable, normal home life.

"We've been able to help a number of such people over what is probably the most difficult period of their entire lives, simply by showing them that Christ is concerned about them and that He is the answer to every problem they have or will have. I'm not in favor of divorce, but it's a very real problem today. We have felt the church has to try to help those who are torn by it."

Rev. Baker has enlisted the assistance of this particular Bible study in a unique ministry.

"I always have several counselling sessions with each young couple I'm going to marry," he said. "For the last session I take them to this particular Bible study and let the people there share the pitfalls and difficulties that can lead to divorce. It's a mighty serious pair that goes out of that room at the end of such a meeting."

Faith Baptist Church does not emphasize all the traditional programs found in the average evangelical church and in some cases eliminates them altogether. Unlike most Baptist congregations they do not insist on baptism by immersion as a condition for membership.

Baker became convicted of that stand in a former charge where a woman who was too ill to be baptized by immersion was converted. "There was no doubting her salvation," he said. "She had a ringing testimony. When she died (which happened in a few days) she would be in heaven.

"It hit me like a sledge hammer. Our church is imperfect, as all churches are, and shot through with sin. Yet we required a condition for membership more stringent than God does for heaven."

When he saw that his position on baptism was impossible to justify through the Scriptures, he urged the congregation to take a less arbitrary position. From a practical standpoint little was changed. Baptism is preached from the pulpit and the pastor urges it as an outward sign of a changed life.

In fact, most of those who come into the church are baptized by immersion as before if they have not already gone through that ritual. If a person has had some other form of baptism, however, he is not required to do so again as a condition of membership.

"We don't vote on members, either," he continued. "You can't find one verse in the Bible that substantiates such a practice. So we take new members in upon a public confession of faith or by letter from another church. I realize there may be a danger in this practice, but I'm convinced it's scriptural and it has produced no problems so far."

Rev. Baker has provided the strong leadership necessary for consistent growth. His application of the small group method of teaching Bible truths brought the church into being. His Faith-Action groups were a forceful method of challenging new and older believers alike to walk closer to Jesus Christ. And his expertise in business (He was training to be an accountant before going into the ministry) helped set the group on a sound financial base. He guided them through a successful building program and was working on a debt retirement plan so they could start raising funds to add badly needed space.

At his urging the board adopted a variation of the small group plan to discuss the budget before it was adopted. The congregation was divided into twelve groups, each meeting on a different night, to have the budget presented and explained.

"We found that it brings out more people than we could expect for a budget meeting involving the entire congregation," Baker said. "And those who come find it easier to ask questions. It's been my experience that the more members the pastor and board can get involved in the business affairs of the church, the better it is."

One of the men in the congregation spoke of the way the pastor got him started working in the church.

"I really don't know how it happened," he said. "Knocking on doors is entirely foreign to my whole personality. I never thought I could do it, even if I wanted to. Before we started going here I wouldn't even have helped with such a small thing as serving Communion. Now the pastor's got me doing visitation, follow up, serving Communion and all sorts of things I didn't think I could do."

While Baker's leadership is not dogmatic or dictatorial, he is able to guide individuals into avenues of effective Christian service, as well as in guiding the policies of the congregation.

o   o   o

Appalled by the lack of biblical knowledge some of the Sunday school teachers evidenced, Baker went to Madison, Wisconsin, to take part in the Lutheran-developed Bethel Series. Back in Fort Wayne he offered the difficult course to his people as a method of teacher training.

"It isn't a course on theology," he explained. "It deals with an overview of the entire Bible. It helps the student know what the biblical narrative is."

It is a taxing course with two and a half hour weekly sessions under the teacher who has gone through a period of special instructions for implementing it and eight to ten hours of homework each week. Faith Baptist Church had 28 enrolled in the course, making it the largest single class in the entire country to date.

"It has been a great experience for me and for the teacher-trainees who have gotten involved," the pastor said. "In the fall of 1974 two members of my class started teaching the course at the congregational level. This is what I'm really concerned about. We have to make our people acquainted with the Word of God."

They have never held an evangelistic campaign and the minister seemed to doubt that they would do so in the foreseeable future. He had 86 of his members working in Sunday school, on the church board and in various small groups. And they were averaging almost 100 new members each year.

"That's about as many as we can assimilate if we're going to do an adequate job of follow up," he added. "Our program of small groups is producing new converts and the people don't seem to want evangelistic meetings. (We took a vote on the subject not long ago and it failed to carry.) So, why not stay with what we have?"

Averaging less than 200 in attendance, the Sunday school is not among the stronger programs in the church. There has been a lack of adequate space, for one thing, and it has been difficult to get well-trained teachers.

"That may be because our work is so new and has been built largely of people with little or no contact with evangelical Christianity, which means that many are lacking in biblical background."

The new building will take care of the problem of space. The Bethel Series, coupled with the Faith-Action groups and sound Bible preaching, should in time adequately train the laity to teach.

Pastor Baker saw the need for a nursery school in the area and convinced a majority of the people that they should start one, using their facilities for it during the week. They now have 170 enrolled in the nursery school with 15 or 16 staff workers, including the teachers, with 20 or more children on the waiting list.

The nursery school has been a means of bringing several families into the church. They first brought their children to the nursery and because they indicated no church preference on the enrollment card, Baker was free to call. Another family felt drawn to the church, themselves, after their first contact through the nursery school.

Although it may seem like heresy to some, there is no mid-week prayer meeting at Faith Baptist Church. To some extent the Faith-Action groups take the place of the more common weekly prayer meeting.

"I used to be greatly disturbed by the poor attendance we would have in my former charges on Wednesday nights," the pastor related. "People would flock to the business meetings and vote, almost unanimously, to keep the prayer meeting in operation, even though they never attended a meeting themselves.

" 'We want the light on in the church on Wednesday night,' " they would say. But that was always for someone else. They themselves never were able to attend during the week. So we had the same pitiful handful of the same older people week after week. Here, we don't have it and I don't believe the church is the weaker for its absence."

On Sunday evening the people get together at 5:30 for group meetings for all ages. At 6:15 they have a snack time or a potluck supper. When we were there one group was studying the book of Acts. Another was learning how the Bible came into being. All the groups were led by the laity. At 7:00 to 7:30 they have a vesper service.

"We want the people to have an opportunity to get better acquainted with each other," Rev. Baker informed us.

When we finished work in Fort Wayne, a number of factors that helped make the church effective began to stand out. We were beginning to see the importance of love on the part of the people for Christ and each other and programs, such as the Bible study for divorced persons, that are specifically aimed to meet the needs of the people. Yet there was one principle that was more in evidence than all the others: *Faith Baptist Church* is built on a strong Bible emphasis.

That is a claim most evangelical congregations would make, but the entire program at the Fort Wayne church is built around the Word of God. The visitation carried on by the pastor and concerned laymen is aimed at recruiting couples for Inquiry groups. There are Faith-Action groups for believers—and both are Bible studies with a differing emphasis. Sunday school teachers are being trained by the rigorous Bethel Series, and the pastor's messages are grounded in the Word.

As we left the city we were sure we were unlocking the door to one of the key principles for building an exciting local ministry.

4

Hillside Church, Armonk, New York

Before we went to New York to check the Hillside (The Christian and Missionary Alliance) Church we knew that the Neighborhood Bible Studies had played an important role in the growth of the congregation. Their story was somewhat similar to that of Faith Baptist in Fort Wayne, yet there was an important difference. The Indiana church makes a determined effort to reach couples by getting husbands as well as wives involved in their Inquiry groups.

We knew the format used by Neighborhood Bible Studies. Their groups meet in homes during the day and are designed to reach the housewife. It is far from uncommon for a local church to be more effective in reaching women than men.

Hillside presented a paradox. Although the Neighborhood Bible Studies had been the underlying force behind its outreach into the community, women did not dominate the scene. The percentage of men in the congregation was substantially the same as the Fort Wayne group had. We found that intriguing and were anxious to learn how they were able to manage it.

In 1965 when Rev. Roland Coffey came to Armonk from Akron, Ohio, to pastor the church, there was no formal membership and the average attendance on Sunday morning was 92. Eight years later, in 1973, there were 121 members°, 20 of which were added in that year, and an average attendance of 240. On Palm Sunday, 1974, there were 342 present and on

---

° Membership is not stressed in the Christian and Missionary Alliance denomination, so those figures are consistently far below attendance figures.

Easter more than 400 (in two services on Sunday morning). In addition they had started a new church a dozen miles north of Armonk three years before, taking 70 from their group to provide the nucleus for the new congregation. Today the new work averages 120 or more in attendance on Sunday morning and is growing steadily.

The pastor was concerned about moving east when it became apparent that the Lord was calling him there. He didn't doubt the call, but he knew Westchester County was the corporate headquarters for many of the nation's largest manufacturing firms and had one of the highest concentrations of executives to be found anywhere.

It didn't ease his concern to find that the county was one of the wealthiest in the entire country, and Armonk stood close to the top of the list of communities with the highest income per capita. At the time he moved there the average salary was more than $20,000 per year and individual salaries spiraled upward to more than $200,000. He expected the place to be a hot bed of materialism and liberal thinking.

"I knew the church was quite small," he explained, "and I wondered how the gospel would be accepted by those who were so obviously affluent. I soon learned that the same sort of sins and many of the same problems that plagued us bothered them too. There was the same spiritual hunger, the same groping for the meaning of life and something stable to cling to. And when they trusted Christ as Saviour there was the same transformation."

The struggling work had something else going for it, however, that he was only dimly aware of. It was just forty minutes from Dobbs Ferry where Misses Kay Schell and Marilyn Kunz, the founders of Neighborhood Bible Studies, made their home. At the time Rev. Coffey assumed the pastorate in Armonk the women had organized two Bible studies in that sprawling town. They had touched the lives of several women but gave no indication that their number would increase dramatically.

"And even if I had known they would grow in size and effectiveness," he told us, "I would not have placed any importance on them as far as the church was concerned. I knew that the Bible studies, as a matter of policy, could not recommend one church above another."

Yet Hillside was in a unique position. It not only furnished most of the leadership for the groups, it was the only evangelical church in the immediate area. Sooner or later many of the converts found their way there.

The minister saw the Bible studies as an effective means of evangelism and encouraged the women of the church to take part, even before he saw that Hillside would benefit directly. When a group grows to 12 or 15, or when all the members are believers, it is the policy to divide and seek new women to fill each group. By this means the number of Bible studies has increased steadily until now there are 25 in the area, involving some 250 women.

The genius of the 'Neighborhood' approach, according to Coffey, lies in the fact that the responsibility for leading the discussion is passed around so everyone takes her turn. It is simple, since all the leader has to do is read the questions, but it does cause her to study harder than she might otherwise.

"The mature believers in the group provide a subtle type of leadership," he said. "They guide the discussion so it stays on the subject and they provide sound, scriptural answers if the women seem to be reaching unbiblical conclusions."

There is a great deal of sharing in the meetings when the girls become more intimately acquainted. They often tell how they have reacted to their husbands or children and ask for prayer.

If there is any one guiding force behind the Bible studies that are doing so much to build Hillside Church, it is *love*. Love is the factor that keeps the women bringing their unsaved neighbors week after week and praying for the new converts or anyone with special problems. They have love for each other and for Jesus Christ.

Newcomers feel this love the first time they attend a meeting. Strangely enough it doesn't have to be expressed. It is just there—in the way the girls respond to a problem shared by one of their group; in the eagerness with which they pray for each other and are willing to help someone in need.

"The fact that the women in the Bible studies love their unbelieving neighbors has made it possible for me to conduct my ministry in a way that I am convinced is scriptural," the pastor told us. "I don't accept the responsibility for doing all the soul winning. I feel it's my job to encourage and nurture that love for the non-Christian and to train and challenge our people to share Christ with those they meet in their daily lives.

"Take the Bible studies as an example. There are 25 of them. At least 250 women are getting together once a week to study His Word. Almost every Sunday someone will come to me, their voices trembling with excitement. 'You'll never guess who I was able to witness to yesterday,' or 'Pastor, I've got to share this with you. I was able to pray with my best friend this week.'

"If I were to try to do the work alone I could never accomplish, in two or three lifetimes, what my people are doing. They are the ones who are getting results. I simply do what I can to direct their efforts and keep them on target."

Contrary to the attitude of some conservative ministers, Rev. Coffey feels an obligation to be involved in the affairs of the community. If it's good for IBM and some of the other businesses to have their people community-minded, it's good for the church and the work of Christ, he says.

With the approval of his board, he has joined the local Rotary Club and is active in the Little League program. He also takes part in school functions, serving on committees and even assisting the football coach by helping to coach the line.

Rev. Coffey was introduced to the high school football coach at Armonk not long after he (the minister) moved into the area. As a result of that introduction he was asked to pray with the local team before each game. Then, because he had played the sport in high school and college, the coach asked him to be assistant line coach.

"It was a big responsibility," he said. "And it cost me two hours a day all through the season. Still it has given me a wide-open door as far as the school is concerned. That contact has made it possible for me to get some of the kids interested in the church."

His oldest son, who graduated from high school in 1974, was the quarterback of the football team and captain of the basketball team. Three of the starting five on the basketball squad in 1974 were active in the church, and so were four of the starting five of the junior varsity team. According to the pastor a large number of those out for sports at Armonk High would call Hillside their church home.

Last Easter Sunday morning a youthful athlete appeared at the sunrise service. It was the first time he had ever come that anyone could remember. The Sunday following Easter he was in church at both the morning and evening services. At the special meetings that began the Sunday after Easter he came forward and received Christ.

"He's solidly converted," the pastor told us.

Three years ago the church was faced with a minor crisis. They had reached the saturation point as far as facilities were concerned. There was no space for new Sunday school classes and those they had were virtually crowded to capacity.

If they were to avoid losing people because of overcrowding, they would have to build. Only there wasn't time for that.

"I've seen the statement by experts in church growth that a congregation must start to increase their facilities when attendance reaches 80% to 90% of capacity," the pastor related. "If it doesn't, attendance will fall off. We were already beyond that point so we were in a critical situation. It was then that God laid the Mount Kisco area ten miles north of Armonk on my heart."

He began to write down the names of those who lived in the area to the north. There were 70 of them, a fine beginning for a new work if the board decided to move in that direction. They would be losing a number of Sunday school teachers and board members, a third of their missionary budget and a fourth of their general budget. That was a sizable sacrifice for any church. But the more Coffey prayed about it the more convinced he became that it was the thing to do.

The board was as excited about the prospect as the pastor.

The course of action was decided in the spring, and in September those involved had the groundwork laid and were starting cottage meetings. In October those who were moving to the new church stopped giving to Hillside and began to put their offerings in an escrow fund to build up capital for launching their new congregation.

There were some interesting developments. Although a sizable portion of both the general and missionary budget was lost to Hillside beginning in October, that month proved to be the largest, financially, the mother church had ever had. November exceeded October and December exceeded November. At the same time the new work was self-supporting, and has been since the very beginning. It has never had a subsidy of any kind.

Choir members left but Hillside gained even more in the months immediately following the removal of the group that formed the new church, so in the end their choir was bigger than before. The organist left and many thought the position would be one that was difficult, if not impossible, to fill. The first Sunday the former organist was gone a black family began to attend Hillside. That afternoon the wife called the pastor and asked if it was true that their organist was attending the new church.

"I have my Master's from the Julliard School of Music in pipe organ," she said. "I'd love to serve the Lord as your organist if you would have me."

"We discovered through that experience that we had made no sacrifices at all," Coffey told us.

Even though the new church was started with 65 or 70 of their people, in a few months the empty places were filled and the ministry at Hillside was going forward as though there had never been a break.

When Pastor Roland Coffey came to Hillside 80% of the people who attended the church lived more than five miles from the building and drove in to the services. Most of those still attend, if they are not involved in the new church, but the newer people live closer to the church. The majority today are living within a five-mile radius, making it a neighborhood church.

"I guess it's what we would expect," the minister went on. "The Neighborhood Bible Studies have brought in so many more people in this immediate vicinity."

At present the congregation is considering another new church in the area south of Armonk. Again they would lose a sizable group of people with a corresponding loss in revenue. The only hesitation at present is because there doesn't seem to be the intense desire on the part of those who would be leaving to start a new work.

o   o   o

When we were in his study getting our recorder set up for the interviews, Pastor Coffey protested that he didn't know why we would come to Hillside. They really didn't have a vital, modern program involving the newest methods of getting people out to services or active in the work of the church. Their Sunday school was small, he said, and at the time was hedged in by a lack of space. They operate no buses and have no plans for any. There is no visitation program and even the youth activities are somewhat limited.

"For a while we were long on activities," he explained. "We had swimming parties, roller skating nights and lots of things doing for the kids. I don't find anything wrong with a program like that. Maybe that was what it took to get the kids out nine or ten years ago. But today we do very little of that sort of thing."

When the kids meet on Wednesday night, 30 or 40 senior high kids, they have a time of prayer first and then a Bible study.

"We don't even have a youth pastor, as such. Dave is an assistant pastor with a special ministry to youth, but his other duties are fully as important as his work with the kids. Some in the field would say you couldn't get kids to come out with a program such as we have. But they do come. And on any Sunday morning the first five rows or so are filled with them. We'll have at least forty out every Sunday. I wouldn't say that's too bad for a church the size of ours."

We had to agree with him. We had been in works far larger who had a much lower percentage of youth in relation to the adult attendance.

Visitation can be the crux of a successful work in many places. We had seen it in churches all over the country in our research for this book.

"It isn't because we don't believe in visitation that we don't do it," Pastor Coffey continued. "It would actually hurt the ministry of the church in the Hillside area. There is a zoning law in Armonk requiring that each house be built on at least a two-acre tract of land. The area is heavily wooded and the houses are secluded. The people who move here want privacy and don't take too well to uninvited guests.

"I'm sure we would find many of them gracious if we called on them," Rev. Coffey told us. "But I also know the people here well enough to know that their resentment would build. For that reason we have no intention of ever launching a visitation program."

Apparently they don't need one. They have an average of

five to ten visitors each week at the Sunday morning service. (Although close to New York, the area is actually rural.) The pastor writes a letter to those people after the first visit, thanking them for coming and trying to include some personal note to indicate the letter is more than a formality. If the same person comes back a second time, he will make a call to their home.

"If they're here twice I feel they have more than a casual interest in Hillside and I have a responsibility to contact them."

They have a strong Pioneer Girls Club with about 60 girls in it. During the time we were there the pastor received a letter and check for $50 from a couple who have no contact with the church other than the Pioneer Girls Club which their daughters attend.

"We're sending this check because we appreciate the training your church is giving our girls," they wrote.

The Vacation Bible School program is the big event of the summer. It was organized six years ago and had grown to tremendous proportions. Three years ago the recreational program operated by the community and Hillside's Vacation Bible School overlapped a couple of weeks. The following year the recreational director asked the pastor to come and see him.

"I'd like to get our schedules coordinated with yours, Roland," he said. "You guys knocked a hole in our program last year."

In 1973 there were 500 kids involved.

o   o   o

We had been waiting for an opportunity to question the pastor about bringing men into his church.

"Frankly," he answered, "I would much prefer to start with men, but there is one thing I learned long ago. As a pastor I have to start with what I have and build on that base.

"This is one of the secrets of any success Hillside has had. Let me tell you how it works." He went on to relate the story of a vivacious young housewife who lived in the general vicinity of the church.

Pat had been deeply disturbed since the Neighborhood Bible Studies ended an hour before. She had only been to three or four meetings and had looked forward to them eagerly until this morning. Now she was miserable. The women had been talking about what it means to become a Christian. One of them told how Jesus Christ stands at the door of our heart and knocks.

"But He won't violate our will," she said. "We have to invite Him in or He won't come."

At first that was reassuring. She hadn't decided whether she wanted to become a believer. She knew she didn't want to be forced into a decision. Now that she was home and thinking about it a great longing swept over her.

She had never heard anything like that in the church she and George used to attend back home before he was offered an advancement that took them to Armonk, half an hour north of New York City.

As she swirled around the house getting lunch for her pre-schoolers she wished they had gone to church more often. She even wished she hadn't been so indifferent when that preacher called on them a few weeks before. At the time, however, she was not really listening to anything he said. She was only trying to get rid of him as graciously as possible.

Pat wasn't sure why she accepted her neighbor's invitation to the Bible study. She was no more interested than she had been when Rev. Coffey called on her. (The visit had been at her neighbor's suggestion, but she didn't know that.) She likely would not have gone but the vivacious girl from across the street came over with a freshly baked cake and a winning smile.

So she had gone and now she was weighted down with the burden of unconfessed sin.

She couldn't stand it any longer.

Fortunately the women had made it plain what she had to do. She glanced at the clock. The kids would be storming in any minute, complaining about how hungry they were. When she had lunch ready and they were at the table she would become a believer.

At that moment the kitchen door behind her swung open. It must have been poorly latched and was blown by a sudden gust of wind. She spun on her heel and stared at the gaping door. The message it carried was unmistakable. Dropping her hands to her sides in a gesture of complete surrender she spoke aloud.

48

"All right, Jesus, come right in, now,"

Although nothing had been said about attending Hillside Church at the Bible study, she started going to services there almost immediately. It wasn't more than a month until her husband and small children were with her.

Six months later the church was observing Communion and the pastor gave a simple invitation.

"If you are here this morning and haven't received Christ," he said, "I don't know of any better time than now, at the Lord's Supper. Why don't you bow your head and confess your sin and ask Jesus to come into your life?"

There was a brief pause before the service continued. As the elements were being distributed George leaned over to his wife. "Pat," he said quietly. "I just asked Jesus Christ to come into my heart."

Today they have a Christian home and are active in the work of the Lord.

"She is typical of what we see so often in our work here," Pastor Coffey told us. "She was reached through the Bible study. When she became a Christian there was such a change in her life George was drawn to the Saviour, too. He decided he had to have the same thing that made such a difference in his wife.

"A man's wife has a much better chance of winning him to Jesus Christ than anyone else," Coffey said. "At the same time she probably has a much better chance of driving him from the Lord than anyone else. It all depends on her attitude toward him after her conversion experience.

"If she is considerate and loving and patient, letting Christ show through her attitude and actions toward him, he very often will be so favorably impressed he will want what has made such a change in her life.

"I realize that's one of those things that's easier to talk about than it is to do. I also know it's the sort of thing that is better taken when coming from another woman than it would from me. So I put my effort into training the women in the congregation for the responsibility of counselling the new converts. I try to teach them how to feed and guide the new believers in their group through those first important weeks following their conversion. I stress the importance of counselling them in their relationship with their husbands.

"We explain that they should constantly stress the fact that the new converts will be able to reach their husbands for Jesus Christ sooner if they are sweet and considerate and subject themselves to him and his wishes (unless the life-style he insists upon is directly contrary to a commandment of God). We teach the counsellors to urge that everything possible be done to avoid a confrontation between the husband and wife over issues arising from the wife's conversion.

"The Christian women who are counselling are usually a little older and can speak from experience, which lends authority to what they say. And many men come to Christ this way, through the quiet, godly living and testimony of their wives. This is how we bring men into the church." He smiled. "Not much of a secret is it?"

It seemed like a great secret to me. At least we had never come across it being done in quite that way before.

o   o   o

Even though there are 25 Bible studies for women, there are four or five couples' Bible studies that have also been effective in reaching men, but there is nothing exclusively for men.

"Part of the problem is that of geography," Rev. Coffey explained. "Many of our men commute—some having to travel quite far and make a number of transfers. They get home later than usual at night and have to leave earlier than usual in the morning. To be quite frank I don't know how many evening meetings I would attend if I had to keep their schedules."

But there are those who come out for the couples' studies and make decisions for Jesus Christ. Joel and Gayle are good examples. They came from widely differing backgrounds and had been attending a liberal 'compromise' church for a number of years. It seemed strange to those who knew them well that they would even consent to go to a Bible study. But they did and apparently enjoyed it. When they heard of a couples' retreat the church was sponsoring, Joel approached the pastor with the request to attend.

"We're not from your church," he said, "but we'd sure like to go."

Before they returned home that weekend Gayle made a decision for Jesus Christ.

"Maybe I should, too," her husband acknowledged, "but I've

got a few hang-ups about this business."

The hang-ups, the pastor learned later, were intellectual. He couldn't square the Word of God with some of the things he'd learned at the university. The couple continued to attend the Bible studies, and a month and a half later Joel came to Rev. Coffey's office and received Christ.

Although the church is quite small, a remarkable number of people are preparing for Christian service. The work is too new to have many on the field, but there is a couple on the Villanova campus working with Campus Crusade and a second couple, who are not formally affiliated with Hillside, but which they claim as their home church, are ministering in the African nation of Zaire.

One young man is going to a Bible school in Pennsylvania and three others are attending the Christian and Missionary Alliance College at Nyack, New York, preparing for the ministry. One fellow in his mid-thirties recently resigned a responsible position at IBM to go to a Bible college to prepare for the ministry.

His wife was converted to Christ through one of the Bible studies a few months before Coffey moved to Armonk. The husband saw the change in his wife's life and was drawn to the gospel. Five or six years after his wife's decision, he accepted Christ at a missionary conference.

"He is one of those fellows who probably could have been reached in no other way," Rev. Coffey told us. "Only his wife could break through the shell of self-righteousness he had built around himself. It's been a delight to see him since his conversion. He has really taken off in his Christian life. He's getting started a little late, but he'll make a tremendous pastor."

There is no doubt that Bible studies have built Hillside. The rest of the program is much the same as any church of comparable size would operate, except that it is carefully tailored to the needs of the community. When the new building, which is imminent, is erected, seating more than 400 and providing ample Sunday school space, there will be room for continued growth. Even then, if the opportunity presents itself the congregation will hive off and organize another church.

"We're not interested in building Hillside into a huge congregation," Roland Coffey told us. "Our concern is to win men and women to Christ and to nurture them until they are solidly established in their faith."

A new principle was whispering to us from the interviews we had just completed, a principle we were to look for in the other churches we would be visiting: *To be effective a church must be able to adapt to the situation in which it finds itself and to the people it hopes to serve.*

This is what Coffey and the women in the congregation have done so successfully. They accepted the fact that wives were being reached for Christ and counselled them in how to live before their husbands so they too could be reached.

The importance of a strong Bible emphasis on the growth and effectiveness of the local congregation was also underscored. We had seen it in each of the churches we researched.

It was a vital ingredient of the ministry of First Mennonite Brethren Church in Wichita. It was the cornerstone upon which Faith Baptist in Fort Wayne was organized.

As Marge and I discussed what we had found at Hillside, she took a pen from her purse.

"I think we have another principle for your notebook," she said. She added a line to the page reserved for that purpose.

1. ANALYSIS AND EVALUATION
2. STRONG BIBLE EMPHASIS

5

Johnston Heights Evangelical
Free Church, Surrey, B.C.

We had visited the Johnston Heights congregation in Surrey two years earlier, so we knew something about it before our current visit. We both had made a few notes as to what we expected to find. However, little Monica was the one who provided us the key to the success of that unusual, fast growing church.

I first noticed her when I was on the platform with Pastor Ken Lawrence in the morning service. She was small for her eight years and looked even smaller in the wheelchair pulled up at the end of the pew so she could sit with the rest of the family. Her hand reached out to pat the cheek of her younger sister. The other girl scowled her disapproval but made no attempt to move away. Intrigued by the radiance in Monica's face in spite of her withered body, I asked about her when the service was over.

"She has a rare ailment that has crippled her severely and has made her bones brittle," Lawrence advised us. "They have to be careful handling her to avoid breaking an arm or a leg. She's in and out of the hospital frequently, but she's got a glowing testimony."

We were interested in learning more and asked about her as we had dinner with the assistant pastor and his wife. Rev. Rae Robinson told us that she had just been released from the hospital the day before.

"I went to see her Friday afternoon, but didn't know what

room she was in, so I stopped at the nurses' station on her floor and asked the supervisor if she happened to know Monica. The place is so large they seldom know the patients by name."

" 'Do I know Monica?' the supervisor exclaimed, beaming, 'Every nurse on the floor knows her. They'd all be in her room all the time if they could.' "

Aware that Robinson was a pastor she told him the girl had a certain ritual she went through every night and one of the nurses had to be with her to help.

" 'She insists that they sing a few Sunday school songs,' the supervisor continued. 'If the girls don't know the words and tunes, she teaches them. Then she has a Bible story that has to be read to her. When that's finished they pray together. She's the happiest person on the floor—a real little missionary.' "

Later in the week we were visiting a friend who worked in the same hospital. Again we asked about the girl.

"Oh, yes," she said. "I've heard about Monica. I don't work on the floor she's usually on when they bring her in for tests and treatment, but the girls are always talking about her. They say they've never seen anyone so happy. And they all know that she's given her heart to Jesus. She's seen to that."

Lawrence's ministry at Johnston Heights rose out of his own discouragement and frustration at a previous charge and a new personal commitment to Jesus Christ. That and a burning desire to try new methods to accomplish old tasks.

He had gone to his former church in California when it was a tiny handful of believers meeting in a small chapel. He had seen it grow into a full-fledged congregation with a lovely sanctuary, a gymnasium and a two-story educational building.

"At first I was happy with what had been accomplished," he said, sharing some of the dark corners of his life. "I thought I'd done quite well and deserved an opportunity to sit back and enjoy it for a while."

But God wouldn't let him rest.

"My people were, for the most part, fine Christians," he went on, "but when we talked with them about reaching their neighbor for Christ, they would tell me that their neighbor was already a believer. Many of them lived on a nearby conference grounds where they had little association with anyone who was lost.

"They would call me on the phone from time to time and ask if I had been out to hear a certain speaker. " 'Oh, Pastor,' they would say, 'you've got to get out and hear the man who's speaking this week. His messages on the Holy Spirit really blessed our hearts.'

"But nothing else happened. They seemed to spend their time getting blessed, personally, without doing anything about reaching the lost. I should have been able to lead them but I wasn't. Maybe that was because I had so many hang-ups myself."

Then he went to a Pastor's Conference Campus Crusade sponsored at Arrowhead Springs and he came home a changed man.

"I met God in a new way that week and caught a glimpse of what could be done. I was chafing to get at it."

He soon learned that his California charge was not the place where he was to have opportunity to try new methods. He would have to seek a new place of service if he wanted to put his new philosophy into practice.

While he was praying about a move the call to Johnston Heights came. The people there were as ready to embark on a new spiritual adventure as he was. They told him flatly they didn't want the church to be only a place where folks came in out of the weather on Sunday morning.

"We don't know what we want to do," they said, "or what we ought to do. That's why we're asking you to come and be our pastor. We expect you to lead us, only we aren't content to go on the way we have been. We want to *do* something!"

"Virginia and I felt as though we were liberated," Lawrence confided. "We began to see the joy of training and equipping people to serve Christ in their homes, their own backyards and at work. Almost from the beginning we could see things happen."

And with the new ideas a new feeling of commitment and love took hold of the people. The church had been crawling along with an average attendance of 160 in 1967. They jumped to 475 in 1972 and 600 in 1973. From a barely subsistence budget of $18,600 in 1967 it jumped to $86,200 in 1973. No attempt is made to keep records on the number who find Christ through the efforts of the church and its members but it averages more than one a week, for a total of 55 to 60 during the course of a year. Few of those make their decisions at a service. They are pointed to Jesus Christ by concerned laymen in the congregation.

The Coffee House was the first effort of the pastor and his people to reach out into the community and present Christ to those who don't know Him.

"Actually," Rev. Lawrence told us, "it was a turning point in the ministry here. It wasn't so much a method we developed as a philosophy. Until that time we were saying to the world, 'We've got the gospel. Come and hear it.' Now we were saying, 'Jesus Christ loved you enough to die on the Cross for you. Let us come and help you to receive Him and let Him provide the answer to your problems.' "

Kids flocked to the Coffee House during the three or so years. It was operated productively, and as many as 350 to 400 came on a Saturday night. And some made decisions for Jesus Christ.

"This is one area where we did keep accurate records," his wife, Virginia, broke in. "There were eighty-five saved as a direct result of this phase of our ministry."

Not long after the Coffee House was opened a girl who was just two years into her teens made her decision for Jesus Christ on Saturday night. There was trouble in the home at the time and the mother was about to move out. She planned on taking the kids with her. In a desperate effort the morning the separation was to become reality, they went to Lawrence for counsel. He had never seen either of them before. They came because of their daughter's involvement at the church.

After a time of sparring and hostility and resentment, the pastor began to share Christ with them. The father's expression softened.

"I've watched our daughter since she became a believer," he said brokenly. "If Christ can change her life the way He did, He can change mine."

With that he became a Christian. Both parents surrendered their hearts to Jesus Christ. They're still together and both say they are happier than they have ever been.

Pastor Lawrence points to the night they baptized eighteen

kids who had been saved at the youth center as the time when there was a tremendous change in the attitude of the entire congregation. Before that night some of the people liked the Coffee House outreach effort, some tolerated it, and some were opposed because of the class of kids that were being brought into the building. After that baptismal service the Coffee House had the cooperation of 100% of the congregation.

"The kids really looked funny coming up out of the water with their long, stringy hair clinging to their cheeks," he said, chuckling. "But you should have seen the glow on their faces. It was as though we had a visitation from heaven. That night we saw what love can do."

The Coffee House brought other needs to the attention of the pastor and the board than the kids who came there. It was through that means of outreach that Lawrence learned of a family needing food. He asked the congregation to bring food for the hamper in the foyer, so they would be able to help this family and others in similar difficulties. At prayer meeting the following Wednesday night one of the men got to his feet.

"I came into this church when it was still a little mission," he said, emotion breaking his voice. "I've never before heard of our church caring whether somebody goes hungry or not."

The ministry has continued since, quietly and efficiently. When the pastor or the deacons learn of a need, they take groceries from the stock at the church and make a visit in the home. Sometimes there is an opportunity to pray for, or with, the people they call on. When the stock at the church dwindles, the hamper is brought out and the congregation replenishes it.

Word of the concern for people at Johnston Heights Church spread. Occasionally someone would bring a hitchhiker to the pastor's door.

"I picked up this kid on the highway," he might say. "I think somebody like you should talk to her."

There is often a chain reaction to a ministry like that of the Coffee House. A kid starts going there regularly, the pastor, his assistant or one of the laymen gets acquainted with the parents because of the son or daughter and there is an opportunity to witness to them.

Rev. Lawrence had a situation like that several years ago.

The man, a well-liked fire Chief in the area, was violently opposed to the gospel. When a visitation team called on him during a Barry Moore Crusade, he ordered them off the place. The pastor knew about that when he met the chief at a wedding where the latter was Master of Ceremonies at the reception.

"He and I struck it off from the very first," Lawrence told us. "I enjoyed his company and I think he enjoyed mine. He seemed impressed with the ceremony, considering the way he hated the gospel."

A few days after that, the chief had a heart attack at the fire station and dropped dead. The distraught wife wanted to talk to a minister but didn't know whom to call.

"Why don't you get in touch with the preacher who has that youth center?" the assistant chief suggested. "The chief liked him pretty good."

Rev. Lawrence not only had an opportunity to minister to the family, it opened up the entire volunteer fire department as well. A month later he was called on again when the widow's mother died suddenly.

"We've had grateful parents from that group come up to us since," he continued, "and thank us for the change that came into their son or daughter's lives after they started going to the Coffee House."

In many cases a high school kid coming to Jesus Christ was the opening wedge that brought the entire family into church.

But, after a time the kids who were frequenting the place regularly got gospel hardened. They would get hopped up on drugs or alcohol and demand that the gospel music be replaced with acid rock, and they weren't going to have anyone approach them about Jesus Christ and the claims He had on their lives.

"We soon reached the place where we were spending all our efforts trying to hold the building together," Rev. Lawrence confessed, "and were accomplishing nothing for God, so we closed up for a while. It's our plan to open again in God's own time."

An interesting thing happened before the youth center was closed, however. A certain gang of guys came in, drunk as usual, and announced that they were going to tear the joint apart. They went into the men's restroom and wrenched the door off its hinges. Then they ripped out the telephone lines so no one could call the police. Lawrence went out to talk to them and the staff went to the basement and prayed. Finally, at 11:00 the pastor and some of his men managed to get them outside and closed and locked the door. In anger and frustration they tore off the front porch and gave every indication that that was only the beginning of their revenge.

"Then a strange thing happened," the pastor went on softly. "I've never seen anything quite like it in my entire life. The kids who had been causing all the trouble—the ring leaders—began to wander about the parking lot and the others did the same. They were like a bunch of ants who have had an obstruction thrust suddenly into their line of march and for a while were disoriented. The guys wanted to do something but they couldn't. They didn't know why.

"While we were praising God for confusing them and saving our building from further damage, the group began to break up. But before they left, the leaders got the porch railing and the boards they had torn off and began to pound them back into place, using stones as hammers. It wasn't the best job in the world, but they did all they could to right the damage they had done."

Some of those same kids have been back to seminars the church has been conducting. They haven't come to Christ, but they haven't caused any more trouble and their hostility is gone. The important thing is that the staff and the people have demonstrated to those kids that they really care about them.

"We have a program, of course," Rev. Lawrence told us as we stood in the foyer of the church on Sunday morning after the people were gone. "But our emphasis isn't on methods. It's on people. The church has to meet the needs of those it is trying to reach."

Like some of the others we visited with in our research for this book, he no longer preaches against smoking or a list of 'cardinal' sins.

"It's not that I've changed my convictions. I've just seen a better approach to the problem. Actually, I think it is the key to the whole subject of Christian living. Ten years ago I would have been horrified to think that I would one day have a Bible study with ash trays conveniently placed in the living room. My kids used to go up to strangers and say,

'You must not be a Christian. You smoke.' It embarrassed us but we were proud of them, too."

Now Pastor Lawrence preaches love for Jesus Christ and walking closely with Him, making it very plain that one should follow the Holy Spirit's guidance in all things.

"Since I decided to leave the convicting up to the Holy Spirit, I continually have people come to me and give me their cigarettes, saying God had convicted them about their smoking," he told us. "At one time I had eight packs of cigarettes lined up a bookshelf in my study. When people asked if I'd taken up smoking I would say, 'You know, there's an interesting story behind each one of those packs.' I had an opportunity to witness by telling one of those eight stories. A couple of months ago some kid swiped all eight of them, so I started over. I've got four up there now."

As he told the story I thought about the 'Little Church' held in the home of one of the members the night before. It was a Bible study and prayer meeting (one of several) which had replaced the prayer meeting in the church and, incidentally, had almost doubled the number of people involved in the Wednesday night services.

A 17-year-old Indian lad was present who had received Christ as his Saviour the week before. He had been on drugs and alcohol and smoked six or more packs of cigarettes each week. After becoming a Christian he had talked with Lawrence about smoking. It was a real problem to him. He wanted to quit but didn't know if he could.

After some discussion he asked the pastor to pray that he would be able to cut down to six cigarettes the following week. When he came into the home where the Little Church was being held, he was beaming.

"I got by with three," he told the pastor gratefully at the meeting we attended.

Before the group broke up for the night the subject came up again. "I don't know whether I really want to pray that I won't smoke at all next week," the new convert said honestly.

"Well, how about asking God to help you cut down to two?" Rev. Lawrence suggested.

They both thought about that, nodding his agreement.

"You could pray that I'll smoke only two cigarettes next week," he said, ". . . or *one.*"

Instead of making the Indian boy feel that he would be accepted only after he met certain standards of conduct, the attitude of the congregation and the pastor spoke plainly of their love for him. In effect they were telling him that they accepted him as he was and would try to help him as God showed him how he should live and what areas of his life needed changing.

"The whole point is," Lawrence told us, "we have a group of people in America today—a majority I'm afraid—who have no concept of morality. I'll have new converts come into my office and ask if it's a sin to live common law."

Another girl came in with a problem that was staggering to her. She had given herself completely to her last boy friend.

"Now I'm about to become engaged. He's going to give me a ring tonight. As a new Christian I don't feel I should go all the way with my fiance. Then I get to thinking: I gave myself to a boy I wasn't going to marry. Should I deny myself to the boy I really love and plan to marry?"

One couple, who came to the pastor recently for help, were advised by the psychiatrist who was working with them to seek sexual satisfaction outside their marriage.

"With attitudes like this so prevalent," Rev. Lawrence said, "we Christians must get our heads out of the sand and start giving these people answers. Christ dealt with the adulteress and sinners. All too often, we Christians aren't effective witnesses because we don't want to get ourselves involved with the kind of people who need help. We want them to clean up first, but it doesn't work that way. Christ has to come into the heart and begin to work before the change shows itself."

Often the layman himself at Johnston Heights won't lead a person to Christ, but will make an appointment for him to talk with the pastor.

"These neighbors of ours are getting a divorce," he will say, "and I've been talking with them about our church and about Christ and how He can help them. Could I bring them over?"

"What pastor isn't thrilled with a request like that?" Rev. Lawrence asked of no one in particular. "Often it's easy to get such a person to receive Christ. The work has already been done by the neighbor."

While the emphasis at Johnston Heights isn't on program, there are times when the Lord lays a certain ministry on the heart of an individual. So it was with the extensive cassette taping that is done at the church.

It all began when someone at prayer meeting asked that they pray for a girl from the Northwest Territories who had been visiting in the Surrey area the past summer. She had written a letter to the pastor telling him she thought she had made many friends among the people but no one had written to her.

He chided them gently, saying they all, including himself, should be more careful about that sort of thing. Someone should write to her or send her a tape of one of the services. He turned to one of the men in the meeting that night. "You know, Bob, why don't you think about starting something like this as a ministry?"

Although the remark was meant for someone else, those words were an arrow driven deeply into the heart of Mrs. Sheila Schmidt. Bob had been a missionary in the north for a time, but she herself had been a short term missionary, so she knew what it was like to be in a place where it was difficult or impossible to get to services. She knew how she had fallen away from the Lord when she first came to Canada from England shortly after receiving Christ. It might not have happened, she reasoned, if she had had the help from her home church that tapes of the services would give.

Bob didn't accept the challenge but Sheila did. When she couldn't get a good reproduction on the cassette by holding the recorder on her knees she took it into the Public Address box and plugged it into the system. The first tape she sent to a missionary the church supported in Northern Manitoba, and the third to a missionary couple in language school.

"I got back letters almost immediately, telling how much they liked it, even though my recordings were not good," she told us. "The only trouble was that I only had one tape each week, which wasn't enough."

So she began reproducing them by playing the tape on one machine and recording on the other. She sold a few tapes for enough to help defray some of the cost of the tapes she was sending away. And as the letters came in from the people who were receiving the messages telling how much they were helped, interest in the project began to build.

The young lady in the Northwest Territories was a good example. Her husband wasn't a believer and it was difficult for her to maintain a consistent Christian testimony. The tapes encouraged her enough that she sought out a local evangelical church.

Missionaries write that the tapes are a spiritual feast for them, a link with home and with God's people that is a tremendous encouragement to them.

"You'll never know how much they mean to us," one couple in Mexico wrote. "We didn't have to go to language school because of the nature of our assignment, but we don't know Spanish and there are no English churches anywhere in this area. So you can imagine what a real Canadian service means to us."

Some missionary families want the tapes every week, others every month and some every three months. They have to pay such high duty on them, even though they are clearly marked 'used tapes' that they feel they cannot afford more than one every three months.

After turning down the project once, the church has gotten behind it with a small duplicating machine and a recorder of sufficient quality to produce good tapes. They also have a committee of three men to serve with Mrs. Schmidt. In addition there are two or three ladies who go to the Schmidt home each week to help get the tapes ready for mailing. They make 40 or 50 cassette recordings each week and mail them to twenty-three different countries.

The tapes have also been used in other ways. A man we will call Mr. X was involved in an industrial accident and was in the hospital for a number of weeks. The pastor called on him several times and Jim Harder took him two or three tapes.

He was one of these people who are regular in attendance but have a highly critical attitude. When he wasn't satisfied with anything or anybody, he didn't hesitate to let the world know it. And, few things pleased him.

He had been out of the hospital only a few days when he went across the street to see his doctor and was hit by a car. This time he had a fractured hip and was back in the hospital again for an even longer period. The tapes were taken to him regularly, and he heard the pastor and others in the congregation pray for him by name.

He was a Christian but now he let Jesus Christ have full control of his life. The tapes showed him how much the people really loved him.

Harder's wife took a cassette player and a tape to the hospital where three people who called Johnston Heights their church were confined. Every week, for as long as they were there, she took up a new tape.

"They said they would play it as much as ten times before sending it to the next person," Harder told us. "It almost made us weep as we realized how much those tapes meant to them. And of course the others in the ward got to hear them too, so there was an even greater testimony involved."

One woman who runs a home for retarded adults is so confined by responsibilities that she never gets to a service. The tapes of the Sunday services keep her in touch with the church.

"You'll never know what a blessing they are," she said.

A missionary in Germany wrote to thank them. "I'm teaching Sunday school during the service here so I never get to hear a service. I was very low when your tape came. The Lord knew exactly what message I needed. I've been listening to it over and over. . . ."

o   o   o

The church has a Pioneer Girls group of more than 100 girls and a new 'Big Brother' program for providing adult male companionship and contact for boys who are fatherless or in homes broken by divorce.

"That program isn't something we dreamed up," Lawrence told us, speaking of the 'Big Brother' project. "It came to us. In one week we had three different women call to see if there was a man in the church who would be willing to take an interest in her son. When there's a need like that you have to try to meet it."

Near the close of our interviews with him, Rev. Ken Lawrence leaned back in his chair and cupped his hands behind his head.

"Even my preaching is different from what it used to be,"

he informed us. "I used to try to take my people deep into doctrinal points. I'd choose a subject like the omnipotence of God. Now that's important to all of us. I guess I still choose subjects like that at times. Only now the approach is different. Today the meat of my message would be in what it means to me in everyday living. How can it affect my life? How should it affect me?"

Thinking over our stay in Surrey while researching the Johnston Heights Church, it seemed to us that eight-year-old Monica portrayed the feeling of love and concern we found there. We decided the main reason it is growing in outreach and attendance is the fact that it is a church where the people truly care for each other and are concerned about those who are without Christ and are trapped in the snare of sin.

We checked our appraisal of the church with a missionary friend who is living in the area and knows the congregation well.

"It reminds me of something I saw there a few weeks ago," he said.

When the service was over our friend waited for his wife at the front of the church. A boy of seventeen or so came up to a male member of the local congregation who was standing nearby.

"Mr. Harder," the lad said seriously, "I've been wanting to see you to tell you how much encouragement your life and testimony have been to my own Christian life the past few months. Your walk with Christ has been so steady and unwavering, it's been a big help to me. I've decided that if you can live for Jesus the way you do, I can, too."

"I get in a lot of churches on deputation," my friend went on, "but I've never seen or heard anything like that anywhere else.

"I'm sure it's a common thing for a boy of that age to be helped by the consistent Christian walk of an older man he admires. The thing that's not common is that he went to this Mr. Harder and expressed how he felt. He wasn't trying to make an impression. He was honestly putting words to his feelings.

"That isn't unusual at Johnston Heights. The people have such love for each other and for every visitor and new convert that it reaches out and wraps itself around you as you step in the door. They can't remain quiet. They have to express their love."

As we left Surrey for the Vancouver Airport we reflected on the church we had just visited. There were areas that could be stronger. The Sunday school was one of them.

Rev. Lawrence is one of the few pastors we have visited who feels the Sunday school is overrated as a force for Christ. Still, Johnston Heights has a dynamic influence on the community. It reaches out into the main stream of life and touches tangled lives and aching, unhappy hearts with the healing hand of Jesus Christ.

Why were they so different from some other churches we knew? There was only one answer we could think of: *The people really care!*

6

First Alliance Church, Mansfield, Ohio

It was unseasonably cold and blowing snow that April noon when we scurried into a cafe in downtown Mansfield. Our appointment with Rev. William Allen, pastor of the First Alliance Church in that city, was for the following morning. We were in no hurry to get back to the drab walls of our motel room so we ate leisurely, lingering over a final cup of coffee. We couldn't avoid overhearing the heated conversation of the three well-dressed young men in the next booth.

"I've had it up to my eyeballs with those blasted evangelicals like that mother of mine," one stormed belligerently. "And their preachers are worse. Talk to anyone in that whole outfit for two minutes and they've worked the conversation around so they're giving you that guff about having to be 'born again.' It makes me sick."

"I know just what you mean, We live next door to one of those guys."

"As far as I'm concerned they can take that stupid religion of theirs and hang it in their ears."

Not all the people of that grimy industrial town buy the gospel of Jesus Christ by any means, but most are keenly aware of it. And why shouldn't they be? For several years there has been a revival among them that has shaken the First Alliance Church and turned it upside down.

Husbands and wives were reconciled to each other, the bitterness of years of feuding and misunderstandings miraculously erased. Children were restored to their parents, often from

lives of ugliness and deep sin. Church members asked the
forgiveness of fellow church members for wrongs that had disrupted the harmony of the congregation. Men and women who
had cursed God by their words and deeds turned from wicked-
ness and received Christ. And those outside the Kingdom of
God marvelled at the transformations even though they were
bitter in their criticism.

Marge and I had been in Saskatoon, Saskatchewan, in
November of 1971, shortly after the Canadian revival broke
out in that city. So we knew something of what happens when
the Spirit of God is given free control in the lives of men.
And we had heard of the revival that had come to the Mansfield church. We wanted to check it out at the time, but
the press of other commitments made it impossible.

Now we were there.

The revival at the Mansfield church began with a book.
It was in 1965 and Rev. Bill Allen had been pastoring the Alliance Church in that city for eleven years when a slim volume
by Robert Coleman came across his desk, *The Master Plan
of Evangelism.*

He began to read with only nominal interest. After all, the
program in the church he served was well established, attendance at both Sunday services was increasing and souls
were receiving Christ. There was much yet to be done, of course,
but he had no reason to be discontent.

Still, the title of the book gripped him, and as he read,
its theme found rich, moist soil in his heart. The most effective
way for a pastor to reach souls for Christ was to follow Jesus'
example of training disciples. Rather than attempting to reach
the multitudes himself in the three and a half short years
of His ministry, He concentrated on twelve men. He lived with
them, taught them and trained them by demonstrating the
methods He wanted them to use. And in an incredibly short
space of time He prepared twelve, largely uneducated men,
to establish His church throughout the world.

"The theme of that book made sense to me," Allen told
us. "The method worked at the time of Christ. If there had
been some better way He would have chosen it. There was
no reason why the plan wouldn't work now."

Allen was disturbed. There had to be a new dimension in

his ministry. He, too, had to train disciples, to equip men in his congregation to do evangelism. Only he didn't quite know how to go about it.

"I was so burdened I fasted at breakfast time for three weeks, using my mornings to get alone with God and seek His guidance," he said. "I had a list of every man in my church, but that number was too large for my purpose. As God led Gideon to a small number of dedicated warriors, I felt I should begin with a few men who were willing to accept the responsibility I wanted to place upon them."

From the entire membership he chose twenty-three men who seemed to have the dedication his bold new program required. Most were in their twenties or early thirties. All twenty-three came to the chicken dinner he held for them one evening and listened with concern as he laid bare his heart. He told them he wanted a small group of men who were dedicated enough to make sacrifices to serve God. He would give them special training in conducting home Bible studies and they would have a time of prayer together.

He challenged them to stand with him for a six months' period. They would have to agree to do three things: (1) Get up half an hour earlier than usual from Monday through Friday and spend that time in prayer. (2) Meet an hour after the prayer meeting on Wednesday night for a special training course on winning souls for Christ. (3) Meet an hour earlier on Sunday evening before the service, for prayer.

Twenty-one of the twenty-three men accepted the challenge. The other two decided they didn't want to start something they would be unable to finish.

"I know it's a good thing," one of the two said frankly, "but I don't have what it takes."

Two years or so later his daughter ran away and got married. He came to the pastor's office, deeply disturbed.

"You remember that night when you challenged us and I didn't accept the challenge?" he asked. "That's the reason this happened. I knew what God wanted me to do but I turned my back on Him. As a result I began to grow colder spiritually and it was reflected in my family. That was where I failed God."

Pastor Allen was quick to say that he himself made no such judgment of the matter. He was only repeating what the distraught father had said to him.

At the time the men in the group began to meet for prayer and training, the pastor launched a series of simple Bible messages. They were on some of the basic fundamentals of the Christian faith; the new birth, the evidences of grace, the inspiration of the Scriptures, and the second coming of Christ. They were so simple a child could understand them.

But Rev. Allen did not stop there.

He had the outlines of the messages, together with the illustrations, typed and printed in the bulletins so everyone in the congregation could follow the sermon. On Wednesday nights he used the same messages to train the men.

"We would go over it in the first part of the hour together," he said. "The men would study it, and then one person would get up and teach it or talk about it. When they went out to their own home Bible studies (which were also a part of the program), they were well prepared to teach the lesson."

Nothing spectacular happened by the end of the six months' trial period, but there was a spirit of love and harmony among the people and a deep sense of expectancy, as though everyone knew something was about to happen. The experiment ended the last of April and by August there were twenty-six new families who had been won to Jesus Christ and came into the fellowship of the church.

o   o   o

Organized in 1916 as the independent Grace Tabernacle, the church had affiliated with the Christian and Missionary Alliance in 1943. Thirteen years later Rev. William E. Allen moved to Mansfield as their pastor.

Two new congregations have been started by the church. The first in 1961 at Westwood when they sent 96 members from their own group to form the nucleus. It was not an easy decision to see them go. In addition to losing a sizable group of members, they had to give up their own assistant pastor who was to take over the new ministry, and they had to help buy the land and build a place for the new group to meet.

"We were averaging 22 in our choir at the time," Pastor Allen recalls, "and 12 of them were leaving to go into the work at Westwood. I could see our Easter morning service with 10 in the choir loft, but when I got there we had 32. The only explanation I have is that it's divine mathematics. Whenever we have given out, God has poured in. We never lose by giving."

The Westwood Church now has an average Sunday morning attendance of 150, and when we were in the area the church was experiencing a real revival in the college age group.

In spite of the members that left to form the new church, the First Alliance continued to grow and its outreach increased. The pastor began to teach a home Bible study near Bucyrus, 24 miles north of Mansfield. It soon grew from 12 to more than 100.

A man who was known as the wickedest individual in the county met Jesus Christ as a result of those studies. The police across the state were well acquainted with him. They had him and his buddy in jail at least half the time. He was the ringleader of what is still regarded as the biggest riot Ohio ever had, one that brought out the State Police and caused many injuries before it was put down. On another occasion he whipped six members of a motorcycle gang, single-handed. His wife called him "Satan," and with good reason.

Then he received Jesus Christ and his life was transformed. Everyone in the area knew what had happened to him. A man doesn't change from brutality and lawlessness to ushering in church without causing a certain amount of talk.

Couple conversion stories of that sort with the community-shaking revival that was to follow and it was no surprise that the men we overheard in the cafe were well acquainted with evangelical Christianity and what it stands for. There would have been something wrong with them if they hadn't.

In 1970 the Bucyrus Bible study group became the nucleus for organizing another church. Again the Mansfield congregation bought a tract of land, this time six acres, and a parsonage. The new pastor was a young man from the congregation who came to Christ under Allen's ministry and was serving his first church in Westfield, Massachusetts.

Today they have a new building that seats 250 and an average attendance of 180. The same spirit of revival that descended upon Mansfield has hit them as well.

The Mansfield church lost at least 100 people in one Sunday to the new work but in five months they were replaced by others. Today the congregation is crowded out and a committee is meeting with an architect, working out plans for enlarging the seating capacity of the balcony by 100 and building a two-level addition 60 feet long. At the time of our visit they were averaging 750 on Sunday morning and 450 to 500 on Sunday night.

"When the new addition is filled, we'll have to decide whether to start a third church somewhere in the area or go to two Sunday morning services," Pastor Allen told us.

According to Rev. Charles Holmes, who grew up in the church and was brought back to serve as assistant pastor, they have 51 young people in Bible college at the present time and about 50 missionaries from the church.

"And a good number of those in school now have indicated an interest in full-time Christian service," he said. "I don't know how many will follow through but there will be a number of them."

In 1961 Pastor Allen started a Business Men's Prayer Breakfast. He went to 33 of the leading business and professional men in the city and invited them to the Friday morning breakfast. They all agreed to come to the first one, but made no commitment to attend more than that. The congressman from that district, who wasn't a believer at the time, was asked to have a part in the program, sharing what the Washington Prayer Breakfasts had meant to him.

"It was completely out of character for me to invite him to speak," Rev. Allen related. "I would never have asked someone who wasn't a Christian to share the platform. It had to be of God."

With the congressman as a drawing card, all 33 of the men came out and the resulting publicity got the prayer breakfast off the ground. Interestingly enough the congressman received Christ as his Saviour not long afterwards as a result of the Washington meetings.

As a result of the prayer breakfasts the last twelve years, 68 businessmen have a personal relationship with Jesus Christ. Although the pastor is careful never to mention his church, many of those men are now members of it and were active participants in the revival.

He also asked the church board to buy newspaper space so he could write a weekly column presenting Christ to those who don't know Him. He told us of one man who came to see him on Saturday morning after reading an article on the new birth that Allen had written for the Friday paper.

"I've taught Sunday school. I've held offices in my church and have been as active as anyone could be since I was a kid," he exclaimed. "But if what I'm reading in this article is true, I'm not even a Christian."

Before he left that morning he was a new person in Christ. He still belongs to the church where he has always attended, but his son and daughter and their families, who are now believers, have joined the Alliance church and are active there.

"I counted up not long ago," Rev. Allen said, "and learned that we have a minimum of 60 families who are in our church who came through the weekly newspaper column. Only last Sunday a new family visited the church and I asked who had invited them. They said they had been reading our column in the paper."

The Mansfield church has been active in many areas, and with excellent results, even before the revival.

"In fact, for five years we thought we were experiencing revival," Allen remembers, "until the real revival came."

During that period one of the men of the church heard a Baptist pastor from Toronto tell of an hour-long Saturday night prayer meeting a group in his church had. They prayed only for the presence of God in the services the next day. Ed Andrea suggested that they have such a prayer meeting in their church. Although Allen was cool to the idea (he felt they already had too much going on), the layman was so persistent that he told him to go ahead.

Only a few came at first but soon the number grew to 12 or 15, and at times there were as many as 20 asking God to bless and use the Sunday services.

A few months later (October, 1971) Allen was convicted of the fact that he had eaten so much at a smorgasboard luncheon in Chicago that he was miserable and couldn't concentrate on the messages. He was overweight at the time. Silently he made a covenant with God to lose weight for His glory.

At the next Wednesday night prayer meeting he felt led to ask for confessions of sin rather than testimonies. He began by relating his experience in Chicago and a few other things

God had been speaking to him about.

One of the elders stood when the minister finished and asked the forgiveness of the congregation. He had been doing a lot of carpentry work around the church and was bitter because he didn't think it was appreciated. Others followed his example.

"That night was precious to all of us," the minister continued. "The revival didn't start then but God was preparing our hearts."

Then the last Sunday night in December Ralph and Lou Sutera (whose wives are members of the Mansfield church and were the evangelists in Saskatoon at the time the revival broke out there) were home briefly for the Christmas holidays and were in the morning service. Allen asked them to take the evening meeting and share what was happening in Canada.

Thirty-five people came forward that night. The following Wednesday night Ralph Sutera spoke again. The meeting lasted for three hours and everyone was sure that revival had come. But they were like men from the prairies on their way west. When they first saw the foothills they mistook them for the mountains. The Wednesday night meeting was a forerunner of the torrent of blessing that was to fall upon the First Alliance Church of Mansfield, Ohio, January 9, 1972.

It was a communion service and for four hours the congregation held the cups while men and women and children got right with each other and with God. The evening service began at seven and lasted until one in the morning.

"Even then our people didn't want to go home," the pastor said.

One of the men came to the platform and before 750 people confessed that he hadn't taken communion for more than ten years. As a 14-year-old boy he got started looking at pornographic literature and hadn't been able to break the habit.

"I've been down to this altar 40 times asking God to deliver me, but He hasn't. A little while ago He told me that if I would get up and confess this before the church He would free me."

It happened, miraculously, and he has been one of the most important figures in the entire revival.

Another man confessed the same sin.

"But that's not all," he continued. "There are two guys

in the department where I work that I've been talking about. I've got to go to them tomorrow morning and ask their forgiveness."

"Hundreds of our people made confession to those they had wronged and asked God's forgiveness," Allen went on. "We have 150 hours of tapes recording confessions and testimony and we're still taping."

Almost immediately the people began to go out in teams, sharing with others the wonderful things God was doing. They weren't planned. "Churches and schools and Bible conferences contacted us to have someone come and tell them about the revival," he told us. "The requests were made known and gospel teams, usually made up of people who had done little or no public speaking, went out to tell what had happened.

"We were all amazed," the minister continued. "People who were so shy and self-conscious they could scarcely do more than give their names in a public meeting, suddenly were bold enough to get up before huge crowds without any trace of fear. You would have thought they were trained in giving a message."

The Sunday morning communion service was only the beginning. The church program was completely disrupted for the next three months or so. They threw the clock away. Nobody knew how long a given service would last, nor did they care.

The story of the revival spread rapidly throughout the country. It also was a sensation right at home. There were articles in the paper about it. For a year the church was on television every Monday night. Pastor Allen would interview those whose lives had been changed by the revival and would close with a brief message. Teams visited at least eighteen churches within the city limits of Mansfield, sharing what God was doing among the people at the First Alliance Church.

At every service during the peak of the revival there would be members of other churches there, curious about what was going on or anxious to fill a need in their own lives. Some would attend their own services on Sunday evening but would rush to the Alliance as soon as they could, knowing the meeting there would continue for a couple of hours or so.

One member of the Alliance church, a banker, came to the altar at the first meeting. He had to get things right with some people, including some members of the church and his own sister. He hadn't spoken to her for more than five years.

The next night he went to a funeral parlor where he unexpectedly ran into her. He asked her forgiveness and they were reconciled, something neither had thought could ever happen. It had such a profound effect on her that she came to the revival, although she was a member of another congregation. She, too, had a meeting with God. She went back to her own church where she told the people about her brother and what had happened to her. Revival broke out there.

"We are seeing people delivered in a moment from emotional problems so deep-rooted it would take hundreds of hours of counselling to help them," Rev. Holmes told the senior pastor at the height of the revival.

One woman, whose husband had spent $10,000 in the previous year on hospitals, doctors and psychiatric treatment for her, came forward to make a new commitment of her life to Jesus Christ. It soon developed that she had hated her mother and father from the time she was a child when they had mistreated her.

"I told her it didn't make any difference if they were 90% wrong and she was only 10% wrong. She should go to them and ask their forgiveness," Rev. Allen related. "God would deal with them."

She followed his urging and did so. She was gloriously reconciled to them and was set completely free.

Teams continued to go out from Mansfield. And wherever they went the revival followed. Hearing the stories of how it spread made us think of the forest fire we had seen in the Canadian wilderness several years before. It was an awesome thing. Pieces of burning bark were ripped from the trees by a raging wind and hurled ahead to touch off new blazes in the most unlikely spots. Sections of lush forest directly in the path were unexpectedly leapfrogged while other areas, thought to be safe, were ravaged by the flames. Although the forest fire was a monster of destruction and the revival a fire of cleansing and healing, the actions were much the same.

The teams fanned out across the country, responding to invitations from concerned believers who longed for the revival to touch them and their churches. When it was too far away to drive the people flew—to Alabama, Texas, Florida and beyond.

After the appearance of three laymen in Huntsville, Ala-

bama, revival came to the church and it was two months before
the minister got his pulpit back and was able to preach again.
It was taken over by laymen, confessing their sin and sharing
what Jesus Christ had done in their lives.

At one church not far from Mansfield, the largest crowd
they had had for a year or two came the Sunday the team
was there. It wasn't because the revival team was there, however. For some time the church had been torn by strife. A
concerted effort had been made on the part of some to get
everyone out so they could have a congregational meeting after
the service and have enough votes to pass a motion asking
the pastor to resign.

"The minister was revived," Rev. Allen told us, "and so
was the congregation. Wrongs were righted, hurts were healed,
and the vote was not taken. Those who came hating the pastor
went home loving him."

At the time teams were going out from Mansfield a total
of 23 pastors from various churches in various cities who were
about to resign and quit preaching altogether, reached a new
relationship with Jesus Christ as a result of the revival and
went back to their churches with a dedication and power they
had never had before.

The intensity of the revival began to taper off after six
months or so, according to the pastor.

"No one can remain on such a high emotional plane indef-
initely," he said. "But the calls for teams keep coming. At
the last count we have been in 430 churches in 20 states and
several provinces of Canada."

Some of the people involved in the revival at the beginning
have fallen away, disappointing those who love them. Others
have been enticed by groups who stress experience above all
else. Most, however, will never be the same again. The cleansing
of confession and asking forgiveness of those they had wronged
added a new dimension to their spiritual lives that gave them
new strength and serenity and power.

If any of the churches we visited prove that there are other
factors than program involved in an outstanding congregation, it is the First Alliance in Mansfield, Ohio. The program
is well planned and vigorously executed, but the revival far
overshadows all that man is doing.

Still, our principles for an effective church stand out in sharp relief, as an examination of the congregation will reveal. The church is strongly *Bible oriented*. Pastor Allen's simple and direct messages in 1965 helped to set the stage for a new relationship with Jesus Christ. Bible truths were brought in terms even a child could understand. Numerous Bible studies were started, which have increased dramatically since the revival.

"The outstanding thing I have seen in the church since the revival came," the assistant pastor told us, "is *the deep love the people have for each other and for those who don't know Christ*. It's a direct result of the confession and restitution that has been done."

Hand in hand with that love is a *deepening love and commitment to Jesus Christ*. That is the only explanation for busy people to go out on teams, week after week, sometimes returning home at five o'clock on Monday morning when they have to work that day.

Allen has exhibited *strong leadership* throughout his more than eighteen years at the Mansfield Church, but it was his concern in 1965 that led 21 men to separate themselves for a special ministry, setting the stage for the revival. It was his leadership that brought the Suteras to speak at the church during the early days of the Canadian revival and made possible the dispensing with time and the regular church program while God was dealing with the people.

It was the dynamic leadership that caused layman Ed Andrea to organize Saturday night prayer meetings for Sunday services, which Allen credits with being the immediate forerunner of the 1972 revival.

The church was adaptable to the needs of the people and the call of God to repentance by providing opportunity for the Lord to work. It was adaptable in providing teams to share what was happening among them so others might have the same blessing.

We visited many churches larger than the one in Mansfield, some with much greater buildings and with staffs that make the Ohio group seem small and insignificant by comparison. However, we visited none that made more of an impression upon us. Perhaps because we, too, were touched by the Canadian revival in a personal way.

When we finished work at Mansfield we were ready to write another principle for a dynamic church in our notebook. The

list had now grown to three:
1. ANALYZE AND EVALUATE
2. STRONG BIBLE EMPHASIS
3. LOVE

7

First Baptist Church, Dallas, Texas

The First Baptist Church in Dallas is a place where everything is done on a grand scale. Look at the figures with us. Their membership has increased by more than 4,600 in the past decade. The gain recorded in that one church is more than 11 or 12 times the number of people in the average congregation. The close of 1973 saw the membership climb to 17,867. That's a little more than a fourth of the entire membership of our own Evangelical Free Church.

And attendance has kept pace with the increase in membership. Most of those who go to church there aren't able to walk around the corner or drive in 10 or 15 minutes. The huge, four-block complex is in the heart of the inner city—a location that has sent less courageous congregations racing for the suburbs in an attempt to stop their sagging membership and attendance.

The total income for all purposes has more than doubled in the last 10 years to an astounding $5,000,000. Funds often seem short according to the business manager, but that is because there is so much designated giving, a practice Dr. Criswell makes little effort to discourage.

We decided to verify the conclusions we had reached at that point in our research by comparing them with what our interviews at First Baptist disclosed.

"If the principles we've definitely settled on check out here," I observed as we went up the steps to the building that housed Dr. James Draper's office, "we can be sure they're sound."

As we went over our material gathered from many sources

in that huge Christian center, we saw that the underlying principles paralleled our new understanding of the factors that make for a dynamic church.

There was no formal analysis and evaluation of the work that was being done, but it went on continually in the department staff meetings and Dr. Criswell's penetrating appraisal of what was being done.

There is a strong Bible emphasis in every area of the ministry.

From the pastor's messages to the Sunday school and youth lessons and the many Bible study groups involving all age levels, the Scriptures are paramount. Converts are encouraged in every way possible to get into the Bible so they will be grounded in their faith.

For seventeen years Dr. Criswell preached through the Word, verse by verse, with few breaks in the long series. A Greek scholar with an earned Ph.D., he reads the New Testament in its original language for devotions regularly and studies a minimum of five hours a day. His interest in the Word came to fruition in the Criswell Bible Institute recently organized and named after him in spite of his strong objections.

His strong stand for the Bible as being literally true has not been without opposition in his own Southern Baptist Convention. In 1969 the Association of Baptist professors of Religion in that denomination condemned his book *Why I Preach That the Bible Is Literally True.* Their grounds: It completely ignored the historical-critical method of Bible study. In plainer language, they did not like the book because Criswell did not accept their liberal interpretation that the Bible is riddled with myths and superstition and error.

This was during Dr. Criswell's first term as president of the convention. It was a stormy period, but Southern Baptist pastors and laymen alike rallied to his defense. He was elected to a second term and the opposition-backed candidate later severed his relationship with the denomination.

Moving to Dallas to take over the pulpit of the late Dr. George W. Truett was a formidable task for young Criswell late in 1944.

"Who's Criswell?" people were given to ask.

He echoed the same question as he stood in the pulpit and looked out over the congregation. It sounded almost ridiculous when he told the people he saw the great auditorium jammed to capacity at the Sunday services and that the day would come when they would have a Sunday school of 5,000. People listened but few shared his exuberance.

Dr. Criswell had already determined the course First Baptist Church should take. It could grow by developing a family centered program with something for everyone: the kids, young people and young families, as well as the older, more mature adults. A large church could be kept warm and closely knit by making it the center of the lives of the people in the congregation.

That was his goal as he moved to Dallas and took up the work. He had not realized he would be challenged so soon, however,

A minor revolution had hit the church of Christ, triggered by racial and financial factors. Blacks poured out of the South, lured to northern cities by the prospect of well-paying jobs. They jammed into rat-infested living quarters in the inner city, trying to make their dreams reality. At the same time the affluence of white workers made it possible for many to move to the suburbs. Everywhere, downtown churches joined the outward rush, buying property and building new sanctuaries closer to their people.

The Board of Deacons at First Baptist Church had considered their own situation and were already agreed that joining the suburban stampede was the only wise solution for them.

But Dr. Criswell did not agree.

The core to his dreams lay in keeping the church right where it was. Much had to be done. The program had to be revamped. The buildings had to be enlarged and new structures put up to house the ministries he already was praying into reality. He continued to expound his philosophy from the pulpit, outlining what he wanted to do and trying to win support for his ideas. His entire future at Dallas was on the line the day they took a formal vote on moving the church. A vote against him would slam him down in a way that would make him ineffective, if he chose to remain.

Just before they voted, the church chairman threw his support to the young pastor. When he asked for all those who backed the plan to remain in downtown Dallas to stand, only two remained seated, expressing their opposition.

Although the victory was won, there was another difficult period a few months later when a motion was made to limit the debt the congregation could assume to $200,000. The proposal sounded innocent enough, but it would have choked off the growth the First Baptist Church was experiencing and would have stifled any effective outreach.

The motion failed. However, there were to be other difficult times in the future, but Dr. Criswell's program was off and running.

Strangely enough the growth of the church was steady in spite of the fact that it ran counter to the nationwide race for the suburbs. Rev. Criswell and his staff began a diversified ministry that was one day to have a day school, Bible institute, and a recreation plant and program that would be unrivalled anywhere. The intense, determined pastor saw the Sunday membership soar and attendance outstrip his visionary 5,000, a monthly payroll larger than that of all but the bigger business firms in Dallas, and weekly offerings that climbed as high as $200,000. (The offerings are transferred to the bank in an armored car.)

When the educational building was completely remodeled in 1956, Rev. Criswell suggested the name be changed to the Truett Building. The board considered the suggestion and made it a reality. Although the elected church officers are not rubber stamps for anyone, esteem for Dr. Criswell and his leadership is so high he is usually given what he wants.

"We might just as well face it," one staff member said candidly (the discretion in omitting the name is ours). "If Dr. Criswell gets behind a project, sooner or later it goes through."

In the 1950s he was strongly criticized for his segregationist views. In the late 1960s he agonized, prayerfully, over his stand and came to the conclusion that there is no scriptural basis for denying anyone the right to church membership because of color. He announced his new decision on the controversial matter to the board in 1968, and they voted unanimously to open the church doors to all. He withheld public announcement until after a vote was taken for the position of President of the Southern Baptist Convention. He was serving his first term in that post and, being eligible for a second term, he didn't want anyone to be able to say he had changed his position in order to gain votes.

Although the official position of the church has changed as far as segregation is concerned and everyone, regardless of race, color or national origin, is welcomed into membership, few blacks have chosen to worship there.

"We have been accused of starting our own day school so our children could be in segregated classes," one of the members told us, "but that's not true. We have black students in our classes. They are as welcome as anyone."

Those who know the church need not be informed that Dr. Criswell's strong leadership has been a strong factor in the success of First Baptist Church. Through his guidance the congregation has seen the needs around them and have developed a many-faceted program to attract special groups.

There is a department for singles, administered by Miss Sylvia Green.

"We have two short of four hundred enrolled," she informed us. They range in age from 22 to 75 or so."

As one would imagine, the younger singles have a full social program. In addition to the usual parties, recreation nights, dinners and retreats, they go skiing and canoeing and hiking.

"Actually," Miss Green said, "we try to plan any sort of outing that interests enough of our singles to make it worthwhile."

The divorced with children have two home Bible studies a week, taught by members of the groups. They have special difficulties and prayer needs not often understood by other singles. Those problems seem to draw them together.

As she spoke we couldn't help recalling our interview with the pastor in Indiana who shared with us his own Bible study for divorced people and his reasons for starting it. Both churches were flexible enough to create programs to meet the special needs of certain groups of people.

"Other churches are doing a far more effective job in the area of helping singles than we are," the director said frankly. "Park City Baptist (the second largest Baptist church in Dallas) has over 700 singles enrolled and they're quite a bit smaller than we are."

o   o   o

We soon learned that no program in First Baptist Church

existed for itself. There is always a ministry involved. It may be evangelistic and it may be for strengthening the believers, but there is always a spiritual reason for the existence of each department.

This is true even of the recreation and sports programs. We were told of one lad who was first attracted to the church by the opportunity to play basketball in a real gym.

"It was something he had never done before and couldn't have done anywhere else," Rev. Dan Beam, Minister of Recreation, said.

Bill, as we will call him, listened to the Word of God for the first time in his life and continued to come back, but apparently wasn't touched by what he was hearing. For several years playing ball was the attraction that brought him to the church. He made friends with Pastor Beam and some of the Christian fellows he played ball with, however. And through their influence his interest in Christ began to build. There was no outward sign but the continual thrust of the Word of God began to disturb him.

"Nobody noticed that, though," Beam continued. "Bill was so quiet and well mannered we all thought he was a believer."

Then Pastor Criswell gave the invitation at the close of a Sunday night service and it reached Bill's heart. He came down the aisle to take his stand for Jesus Christ.

In 1973 six boys who were playing ball with one of the church teams were challenged by the claims of Christ on their lives. Before the season was over they had all made decisions for the Saviour. At the time we interviewed Rev. Beam in April the boys had completed the course of training used in follow-up, were baptized and joined the church.

Susan is a ten-year-old who decided to walk with Jesus Christ at a Junior Retreat where the Bible was first made real to her. The family wasn't Christian and her only contact with God was through the occasional meeting she attended at church. Her parents were in the service with her the next day, having given permission for her to make an open profession of faith in the morning worship hour. The following week she received a letter from the church encouraging her in her decision. A few days later someone from the church called on her and invited her to join a New Members' class for the next five Sundays.

"You'll be taught from the little booklet Pastor Criswell has written entitled *Joining the Church*," she was told.

We were interested to learn that her parents were also asked to attend so they could know what their daughter was being taught.

"We have an obligation to let the parents know what we're teaching their children," Miss Millie Kohn, the Junior Director, told us. "We also like to have the parents come because it gives us an opportunity to present Christ to them, too."

When the training period was over one of the more mature Christian women in the church talked with Susan about the decision she had made and the obligations and responsibilities of being a church member. Again the Bible and its teachings were stressed.

Then Miss Kohn made an appointment and went to Susan's home. She explained the meaning of baptism, the Lord's Supper and what is involved in being faithful. She went over Susan's new relationship with Christ again to be sure she completely understood what she had done in giving her life to Jesus Christ. Before leaving the home the worker from the church directed her attention to Susan's parents, asking them about their own relationship with God. They agreed to go with Susan to see Dr. Criswell before she was baptized. There, in his office, he led them to Christ. Today they are active members.

After having been around First Baptist Church for a time we were better able to understand why people gravitated to it. There was a deep-rooted love among those we met. Even though the congregation is so large it is difficult for small town folks like ourselves to comprehend its size, and though the pressure Dr. Criswell and his staff have to work under must be staggering, a little girl like Susan is important to each of them.

That was only one piece of evidence we saw of compassion and love while we were working there. A little more of the mystery that was First Baptist Church was soon unravelled.

The same love that drew the little girl to Christ is shown in the eight mission churches and one Sunday school the downtown church maintains throughout the Dallas-Fort Worth area. Somewhere in the dusty archives is the record of the other churches that have been started over the years with the active help and encouragement of the big church.

As we sat in his office near the end of a busy day Rev. M. D. Rexrode, the Minister in charge of Local Missions, shared the work of his department with us.

"We have 26 staff members," he told us, "but the *Good Shepherd* ministry is the one I find the most exciting."

As it has been with so many new programs of the church, Dr. Criswell was the first to recognize the need and bring it before the board and the people. The work was begun but there was little success in those early months. It soon developed that those who lived in the area did not want to make themselves a part of the regular church program. So the church decided to develop a program of their own for them.

Before long they had a minister whose primary responsibility was with the people who lived in the scruffy downtown apartments. He devoted special attention to the sections where there were no churches. The response, so poor a few months before, was heartwarming. The *Good Shepherd* program began to grow until they now have six buses that bring the people to their services. There are more than 550 enrolled in Sunday school with an average attendance as high as 300, and a fourth of the baptisms performed at the big church in a given year came from the *Good Shepherd* ministry.

"We have a great deal to be encouraged about," Rexrode said, "but absenteeism is a discouraging factor. We have had most of our success with kids and young people and they aren't the ones who make the decisions as to how the family spends its Sundays. If Dad decides he wants to go fishing or to Fort Worth to visit relatives, the kids have to go along."

On Tuesday nights they will have 150 to 250 youngsters in the church gym—skating, playing basketball, bowling and taking part in the other activities.

"I would guess we have a better response to the recreation program than from any other group the church is sponsoring," Rev. Rexrode told us. "I suppose it's because they are from lower income families and get fewer opportunities for the kind of recreation we provide."

Most of the *Good Shepherd* people find money hard to

come by, but they consistently manage to raise $20,000 or more to meet half the cost of their budget. The balance comes from the Local Missions Department.

"Like I said," Rexrode continued. "We have to get most of our Sunday school teachers from the big church. The people who help us in this way have a burden for the ministry and want to see hearts touched by Jesus Christ."

The *Good Shepherd* program is only one in his area of responsibility. There are others, flung across the city.

Truitt Chapel is one. It is in the heart of West Dallas, an underprivileged area that is rapidly being upgraded with new homes and paved streets that followed close behind the water and sewer systems installed a few years ago. It is somewhat different from *Good Shepherd* in that it is a family type church and is strong enough to provide its own leadership. The people there look only to First Baptist for some financial assistance. They have an average attendance of 70 with a potential of at least 100. One or two Latin American families come occasionally, but the mission church is predominately Anglo.

Meadow Gardens is still another mission, completely different than either of the others. The community in which it is located has gone through the traumatic experience of changing its racial make-up twice in recent years. It used to be totally white but the Latin Americans began to move in. It wasn't long until the Anglos were a minority. Some of the older adults remained but there were only a few of them. Then, dramatically, the scene shifted once more. Both blacks and whites began to buy up homes as they came up for sale. The area, surrounded by blacks, soon became almost completely integrated.

To some degree the church reflects the make-up of the community. The majority of the congregation is Latin-American with a sprinkling of whites and a dozen or so blacks who call it their church home. Although there is no evidence of racism, the blacks who attend the church seem to drift out after a time, to join black congregations. We found this to be true all across the country.

"*Meadow Gardens* will always be a mission," Pastor Rexrode said. "They have their buses to bring in the children, but we furnish the leadership and considerably more than half of their budget."

There is a different arm of the Local Missions Department that reveals the dedication to Christ on the part of the First Baptist Church leaders and much of the membership. *South Mesquite Baptist Church* was organized a number of years ago through the vision of others. Most of the people had low, or lower than average, incomes. However, that didn't stop them from launching a building program financed by bonds. They thought they had the solution to their problems, but financial difficulties developed and it looked as though the building would have to be sold. The board came to First Church for help.

"We couldn't let them be forced out of their building," one of the staff told us. "With the financial assistance and type of leadership we were able to give, they got back on their feet. The work is flourishing."

They had 40 to 50 attending regularly when they approached the downtown church for help. Today they have an average attendance of 200 or more. They have built an educational unit and are soon going to need more space in the auditorium. They now have had more baptisms of new believers than they had in attendance when First Baptist became involved.

The outreach program of the huge Dallas church has some startling figures, including a total Sunday school enrollment of 1700 in the Local Missions Department. They had averaged more than 1100 in attendance for three of the four Sundays preceding our visit. During that month and the two prior months, they had more than 40 baptisms as a result of the program. It is an effective witness for Christ.

o   o   o

No one seems to know with certainty how *Silent Friends*, the deaf ministry, came into being. Some say it was because Dr. Truitt's brother was deaf and the pastor wanted to provide him with a way to worship. Others agree that Dr. Truitt's brother being deaf was responsible for the interest of the church in the plight of those handicapped in that way, but say it was not done for Samuel Truitt's benefit. He was a devout believer, could read Braille and was a proficient lip reader. They say the ministry was launched because of Samuel's concern for his deaf friends. Whatever the reason for its origin, it has provided a tremendous means of presenting Christ to the deaf and their loved ones.

Most of those in this department are disadvantaged only in that they are deaf. They come from normal family situations and are usually brought by grateful loved ones who are appreciative of the help the Silent Friends minister, Rev. Joe Johnson, is able to give them.

Silent Friends has proved to be almost as productive in reaching the families of the deaf as it is with those who are afflicted, although in a more indirect way. Jerry (not his real name) is an example. He himself has no hearing problems, but his sister is deaf. His parents are members of a large church where the gospel is seldom, if ever, heard from the pulpit. Although they now attend First Baptist Church, they came only because they wanted to get their deaf daughter to the church so she could benefit from Rev. Johnson's ministry. Jerry came, too, and it wasn't long until he made his decision for Jesus Christ.

Today the entire family attends regularly.

Jerry is not unique in the way he came to receive Christ. Every department of the Sunday school and most other divisions of the church have their examples of the outreach of the *Silent Friends* ministry.

○   ○   ○

As we set up our tape recorder in the office of Gary Moore, we weren't particularly excited about the contribution the Music Department would make to our research material. We soon discovered how wrong we were. No one at First Church takes the Music Department for granted. More than 1200 people are involved and their choirs have roamed the world.

Moore, who came to the Dallas church two years before, never has less than 17 choirs and often as many as 23. There is a full orchestra rivalling that of most colleges and a vast assortment of duets, trios, quartettes and sextettes in addition to the soloists.

"We have many requests from outstanding vocalists and musicians to come to our church," Mr. Moore told us, "but frankly, we have so much talent within our own groups we would rather use our own people."

The junior high gang has a singing group they call "His Kids." They sing regularly at hospitals and nursing homes in the area and have ventured as far away as Austin to entertain a group of retarded children. A similar senior high group was in the process of organization under Moore's personal direction when we were there.

There is the Sanctuary Choir, which is responsible for singing at the services, while the Chapel Choir, made up of young people, does most of the travelling. They usually take an extensive trip each summer. Then there is the Clarion Choir and a host of others made up of kids ranging in age from preschoolers through junior high.

"We look on our younger groups as an evangelistic outreach," Moore explained. "Kids from unchurched homes frequently sing with us."

The staff often establishes the first contact with a new family because a mother wants her child to have the musical training offered at First Baptist.

Although there are no regulations for those who sing in the children's groups, the church requires that the youth and adult choirs are made up of members.

"It only makes sense," Mr. Moore told us in reply to our question. "How can a guy or a girl sing about the love of Christ if they have never, personally, experienced it?"

The Chapel Choir began its tours in the fifties by venturing into other Texas communities. It wasn't long until they branched out to include Louisiana and a few other nearby states. The response was so gratifying that the trips were lengthened. After the choir completed one itinerary that included Canada, the Prime Minister wrote Dr. Criswell complimenting him on the fine impression the teenagers made. In 1970 they went to the Far East, singing at churches, American Service men's camps and even at a Prince's palace.

"When we're on tour we sing wherever we are invited," Mr. Moore told us. "The only limitation is that imposed by our schedule."

In 1972 they went to Colombia, South America, and in 1973 to England, Scotland and Wales, where the response was enthusiastic. In 1974 they made a trip to the major amusement parks in the country, singing and witnessing.

On occasion invitations are given and the kids go down to

counsel and pray with those who wish to make decisions. Usually, however, the seed is planted and God is trusted for the increase. Not too many make public professions of Christ at their programs.

Undoubtedly the music attracts those Christians who enjoy singing or playing an instrument and may have drawn some to the church by that opportunity to join a musical group. Primarily, however, Mr. Moore is concerned that his department be an active evangelistic tool. It is a means of drawing people to the church so they can be challenged by the gospel of Jesus Christ.

When our work was finished we left the church reluctantly, as though we were leaving long-time friends. We couldn't help thinking of Rev. Criswell's first Sunday service when he made an optimistic forecast of the bright future ahead. How prophetic he was.

Today the membership is more than twice what it was when he began his ministry there, and the Sunday school attendance has reached his goal and more, with a membership of over 10,000. First Baptist Church of Dallas is, indeed, an exploding church.

There are many factors involved in the gigantic growth of the congregation. The dedicated staff is continually appraising its effectiveness and searching for ways of improvement. The Word of God is effectively presented in every activity and department. There is a love of Christ as well as for fellow believers and the unsaved that breaks down the impersonal approach so often found in large organizations. Strangely enough, First Baptist has the feel of a country church. And the program is so diversified there is something for everyone.

Saying all of that, however, does not get at the real reason behind the growth of First Baptist Church in Dallas. There is another principle that was apparant in every interview, in every piece of literature we read about the church. It is stamped indelibly on everything that is done.

The most important factor, from a human standpoint, is the dynamic leadership Dr. Criswell provides.

8

Metropolitan Bible Church, Ottawa, Ontario

John Diefenbaker, former Prime Minister of Canada, tells the story of a small boy from one of the western provinces who was moving east with his parents. Kneeling beside his bed the night before their departure, he concluded his prayers by saying, " . . . Daddy just won the election and we're going to Ottawa. Good-by, God. We'll see you when we get back."

Apparently the lad didn't know about the Metropolitan Bible Church in the nation's capital. 'The Met,' as it is lovingly called by its members, has stood its ground near the heart of the city, strengthening believers and proclaiming Jesus Christ to the lost since its origin in 1931. While other churches in the immediate area have been slowly strangled by a shifting population and the numbing indifference created by a Bible-forsaking ministry, the Met has continued to grow.

In 1967 the church built an educational building to ease the shortage of Sunday school classrooms. Today the Sunday school has crowded every available corner of the building and has spilled out into the neighboring YMCA. (The newly expanded busing program that reaches across the river into Hull, Quebec and the outlying areas of Ottawa has been an important factor in the sudden explosion of the space problem.) And the morning worship services see the auditorium, which seats 900 to 1,000, comfortably filled on the average Sunday.

Pastor Don Jost, whom we met several years earlier when he was a member of the Barry Moore Evangelistic team, hinted of a unique philosophy of leadership at the Metropolitan Bible Church when we contacted him about our visit to Ottawa.

"I know of only one congregation in the United States and Canada that operates exactly the way we do," he wrote. "While the church was beginning to come alive before our leadership methods were launched, I'm convinced that they had much to do with the continued growth. . . ."

We were intrigued by his letter.

It couldn't be that Rev. Jost was referring to another *Criswell* who had appeared on the Canadian scene. That sort of leadership isn't *launched* by anyone. It strides to the center of the arena and takes over. Besides, there were other pastors across North America who display that type of ability.

"It has to be something else," Marge observed. And, as though we might miss it when we went to Ottawa, she wrote in her notes, "Be sure to ask about leadership at the 'Met.' "

She needn't have been concerned. It was not the sort of thing that is easily overlooked. It started shouting at us soon after we arrived in the Canadian capital and went to work.

The church building is in downtown Ottawa. It hides behind a theater marquee on Banks Street just off the Queensway Express, a stone's throw from the charming, age-mellowed cluster of government buildings that house the nation's bureaucratic and political machinery. It was born of a sorry conflict in one of Ottawa's few evangelical congregations in September, 1931, over a problem now all but forgotten.

There is more of the theater in the construction of the building than the marquee, however. The floor is slanted like that of a theater and there is a spacious balcony to increase the seating capacity.

The growth of the church sagged following Canada's entrance into World War II as young men exchanged civvies for the olive green and the whites and the blues of the Armed Forces. Even after the war ended the work limped along. In 1950 when Rev. James Vold became the pastor, Sunday school attendance was an unimpressive 140 and church attendance was correspondingly low.

"Most of us thought the Met was destined to remain a small, struggling church," accountant John Boles told us, "but God had other plans."

"You see," J. H. W. (Bert) Cavey, Sunday school superintendent and in private life the Director of Ports and Harbors for Canada, broke in. "God has blessed our church with sound, effective Bible preaching from the very beginning more than 40 years ago."

His remark reminded us of the statements Rev. Herbert Arnold, Minister of the Pulpit at the Met, had made the night before in response to a question.

"This church has been blessed with faithful, Bible-preaching men. There's never been any other kind in this pulpit. So, those of us who followed them could start building immediately. We haven't had a lot of things to undo and straighten out."

When Rev. Arthur Larson came to Ottawa from the First Baptist Church of Belfast, New York, in 1961, he found a dedicated group of men and women whose concern for the church and the ministry of God was matched only by his own. Delighted, he set to work.

"When Rev. Larson came," one of the laymen recalls, "it seemed as if God was ready to move in our church."

Prior to 1950 Sunday school was held in the afternoon with a disappointing average attendance of 100 to 110. A graph covering sixteen years, beginning with 1950 when the time was changed to the more conventional 9:45 a.m., shows that their Sunday school was far from sensational. The graph line rocks along over the foothills of an occasional good year, only to skid, inevitably, into a valley the next, signifying a loss of ground. There was some improvement over the years but not enough to encourage anyone.

When Rev. Larson came the trend was reversed and a consistent, although unspectacular, climb set in. The 1961 figures are unavailable, but in 1963 the morning worship service averaged 415 in attendance. In 1967 it had climbed to 550, and in 1973 it was a bit less than 1,000.

In the beginning the Metropolitan Bible Church was independent but in 1937 it affiliated with the Canadian based Associated Gospel Churches.

Rev. Jost was right about our surprise at the philosophy of leadership at the Met. For almost a year we had been traveling across the United States and Canada visiting churches. Nowhere had we come across another church where three pastors worked together as a team without having one who was responsible for the activities of the other two.

"Look at it this way," Mr. Jost explained. "Doctors are specialists in particular fields. So are we. Pastor Arnold is the Minister of the Pulpit. Preaching is his responsibility.

"Pastor Morry Worozbyt is the Minister of Visitation and Evangelism. He is not as much at home in the pulpit as Pastor Arnold is, but he's a pastor, nevertheless. His duties are in the area of visitation, personal work and follow-up.

"He's in charge of the Neighborhood Fellowship Ministry in which members of our church family are encouraged to get acquainted with their neighbors who are attending the church. He also supervises the Hotel and Motel Bible Distribution Ministry and the Outreach Ministry by organizing and sending out gospel teams and the church band."

Rev. Jost went on to say that he is the Minister of Music and Christian Education. "I know my own limitation. I'm not enough of a student of the Word to be able to preach with the authority Pastor Arnold can.

"I've done quite a lot of preaching. I even filled the pulpit here between the time Rev. Larson left and Pastor Arnold came. But I'm not really at home bringing messages. I like working with people in Christian Ed and Music. I enjoy television and radio and leading the choirs. Each of us has his field and his responsibilities," he concluded.

We were interested in the mechanics of their staff operation and asked about it.

"Each of us works directly with the lay committees in charge of our particular areas," we were told. "It's up to us to carry out our duties as they direct and as we feel God is leading.

"And there's another thing. The board recognizes each of us as pastors, and so do the people. If a call for counselling comes in to Pastor Arnold and he is unable to take it, the people can be referred to either Morry or me without having the person feel he isn't important enough to have the senior pastor find time for him."

"This sounds great, as something to talk about, Don," I said, "and I'm sure it looked good on paper when it was worked out. But, honestly now, how does it go in actual practice? Pastor Arnold's really the one in charge, isn't he?"

"A lot of people think that, but it isn't the case. He doesn't dictate to me or to Morry. Each of us is in charge of our areas of ministry."

"And what happens if there is a serious difference of opinion between the three of you?" I asked. "What if something comes up that Pastor Arnold feels would harm the entire ministry of the church if it were done your way?"

He had to think about that. "I can't conceive that happening."

Later we put the same question to Pastor Arnold. "I can't conceive that happening, either," he replied. "I might say I find myself very comfortable with this situation. I have the utmost confidence in the two men who are serving with me and I'm sure I enjoy their confidence. Frankly it's a relief not to be responsible for directing their activities."

I repeated the question.

"I honestly don't know what would happen," he said. "I rather imagine my decision would hold if it came to an absolute showdown. . . . " He pulled in a deep breath and grinned. "I hope we never have to find out."

"There is one key to the effectiveness of the Metropolitan Bible Church that's more important than anything else in my opinion," Pastor Jost informed us. "That is the biblical approach that is taken in every situation and problem. It's in the counselling, the Sunday school and youth work as well as the pastor's messages. Actually, there's an emphasis on the Scriptures in every department."

This was not a surprise to us. Wherever we had been where God is working in a mighty way, we had discovered that His Word is at the heart of every activity.

"Another is the strong lay leadership we have," the Christian Education Director continued. "We have some men of outstanding ability and background who have climbed the ladder of success in government circles or the professions or in business. They are completely dedicated and have skills and experience and training that is invaluable."

A number of changes have been made in the organization and administration of the church in recent years. At the time Rev. Jost moved to Ottawa to assume his responsibilities, the Board of Deacons was involved in every time-consuming detail. They decided whether or not a certain missionary should be supported, if the nursery should be painted, or who should be called to fix the furnace.

"They didn't complain," Mr. Jost continued, "but we soon realized we were wasting their time by dragging out our meetings with details. The effectiveness of a highly experienced group was being impaired by an archaic system that threw an unnecessary load upon them."

It fell to the Christian Ed Director to work out a group of committees to make recommendations to the board. The committees would make no decisions, but they did the leg work and preliminary discussion. Matters of small importance could be handled without forfeiting the control of board action.

"We had done the same thing at the Winnipeg church where I served before moving to Ottawa," Pastor Jost told us, "so it was merely a matter of adapting what we had previously worked out."

There has been a marked change in the board meetings.

"Frankly, I used to dread them," one of the men informed us. "Now we go to a meeting, the committee chairmen bring their recommendations and they usually are able to give us enough facts to make it possible to vote quite quickly on all except the most difficult items. We have the time we need to consider important matters. All of that and we get home at a decent hour. It's great!"

This, of course, is exactly what Pastors Larson and Jost intended when they recommended the change in the organization at the Met.

The change to a committee system has had the approval of the congregation from the first. The people were not quite as well pleased, however, when the decision was made two years ago to have each person register his attendance at the Sunday service.

"What're you going to do?" one man who was always present grumbled, "fine us if we miss three Sundays in a row?"

But the reasons for registering everyone were many. The number of filled-out visitors' cards surged. Apparently they didn't feel so conspicuous when everyone filled out cards. It also gave the church a record of those who began to miss services because of illness or disinterest.

"Sometimes," Rev. Jost concluded, "we find out about a real need just by calling on absentees."

"I don't know whether a psychologist would affirm this or not," John Boles said, "but I'm convinced that the easier we make it for people to share their problems with us the more quickly they will do so. If they are filling out the card anyway, they can scribble a note on it or mark a box indicating they would like to have one of the pastors make a hospital call or give them an appointment."

Sunday school at the Metropolitan Bible Church would be considered dull and unimaginative by those in some circles. Yet the Sunday school is thriving.

For several years they operated two buses with uncertain results, but a new thrust increased the number to five. And a recent contest caused their attendance to leap dramatically. They now are operating ten buses, have more than 900 in attendance on Sunday and have had to secure extra classroom space in a YMCA not far from the church.

"I'm convinced we could increase our Sunday school to 1,500 or 2,000 with a little effort," Rev. Jost continued, "but we keep reminding ourselves that these new kids don't know anything about the gospel of Jesus Christ or the Bible. They've never even heard John 3:16.

"We can't put them in classes with kids who have been brought up in the church. We've got to train extra teachers, establish new classes, find exactly the right material and provide space for them.

"We're getting so many who speak only French that we have started two classes in that language and hope to have more. We've called a halt to further recruiting for now. When our efforts are consolidated and we reach the place where we're sure we're doing a good job, we'll hire more buses and go out after an additional 200."

He went on to tell us how the busing program worked along with Pastor Worozbyt's visitation ministry in an effort to reach the entire family for Christ. The parents of five children were recently reached for Christ through the combined efforts of both departments. A woman in the church invited the kids to Sunday school and gave their names to the bus captain who was in charge of the area where they lived. It was at the time of the Sunday school contest. When he called at the home the following Saturday the mother agreed to go on the bus with the children. Her husband, who had been raised in a religious home, was hostile.

"That's who it's for," he muttered darkly. "Women and kids who don't know any better."

The efforts of the church did not stop there, however. A visitation team also called in the home and the men gave their testimonies. Several weeks later the same team made a second visit in the home.

"I've been doing a lot of thinking about what you men said. I want to accept Christ."

On Sunday morning he came forward to publicly confess that he had accepted Christ. After the evening service that same Sunday night his wife joined him in listening to a cassette on the assurance of salvation. Although she had been reluctant to make a decision before, she now recognized the need in her heart and her husband prayed with her.

"That," Pastor Arnold told us, "is what makes all of this worthwhile."

The Honeymooner's Sunday School class was set up to reach the newly married and draw them into the activities of the church.

"There were fifteen weddings here last year," Rev. Jost explained. "And, once they were married, we saw a definite drop in the regularity of their attendance at services."

Besides, there were special problems facing the newly married as they mastered the art of living together in harmony. So the class was organized. Don Robertson, a tall, handsome young Christian who is happily married and has a lovely family, was given the responsibility of teaching them.

As Pastor Jost told us about it, one of the principles we had discovered as important in an effective church flashed through my mind. I wrote the word at the top of my notebook. *Adaptability.*

This was indeed an important cog in the work of the Met. The program was kept flexible enough to include new activities to meet the needs of the people.

"Bert Cavey has been Sunday school superintendent for many years," we were told. "When there has been a gain in attendance or effectiveness in that area, it has usually been because of Bert."

The principle of leadership came to mind. The philosophy of having three pastors with equal positions and equal responsibility was unique, but there was more to the leadership of the Metropolitan Bible Church than that. The leadership furnished by laymen in the church contributed in large part to the growth and spiritual depth of the congregation. Men like Bert Cavey and John Boles, to name only two of many, have had important roles in the ministry of the 'Met.' Nowhere is the lay leadership any more evident than in the Pioneer Girls and Christian Service Brigade programs. Both Boles and Cavey were excited about what is being done in those areas.

"Pastor Worozbyt was on the staff of Brigade for seventeen years before he joined our staff," Bert said. "I don't know whether or not that has had anything to do with the fact that the work has been so effective here. He has made the Met his church home since he moved to Ottawa and has helped us with Brigade all along."

"That's right," the other broke in, "but don't forget, Bert. You were one of the men who started Brigade. And your boy got the first Herald of Christ award in Ottawa." He turned back to us. "We've got a fine bunch of leaders who are so excited about Brigade they want to keep it in operation all year. We've had eight or ten boys earn the Herald of Christ award, the highest honor given by the organization." We were also reminded that no other group in the country had as many boys earn that rank.

A lad we will call Steve is one of the products of Christian Service Brigade at the Met. He was won to Christ through the program and went on to Bible school where he made an enviable record, both scholastically and spiritually.

"He's one of our keenest kids," the school president said of him.

His home life was far from ideal and he could well have become a belligerent dropout of society. But an interested bus captain got hold of him and brought him to Sunday school where he heard about Brigade. He was then drawn into the organization, and a leader who understood his need helped him to receive Christ.

"Both Pioneer Girls and Brigade have had an amazing effect on the lives of our kids," Pastor Arnold said.

The average Sunday morning will see 170 young people between the ages of 13 and 17 in the service and 110 or so of college and career age.

"I've been disappointed that many of them are not involved in our youth program," Pastor Jost told us. "I suppose that points up a certain weakness in our youth program or we would have a higher percentage of them. One of the problems is that of time. Since we started our TV program a couple of years ago, I haven't been able to spend as much time with the youth of the church as I should."

Still, at a recent retreat for the college and careers gang Rev. Jost was asked to speak. There were three different groups represented: committed Christians; believers who had never acknowledged Jesus Christ as Lord and Master of their lives; and those who had not received Him as Saviour at all.

"It was one of those rare occasions," he went on, "where I've been sitting at a campfire where some kids were lighting cigarettes while others were giving their testimonies."

There was a great deal of praying for those who needed Jesus Christ, and it wasn't long until the believers began to witness to them. Some got so strongly under conviction they left the camp on Saturday night.

"They couldn't take any more," the pastor told us, "so they blasted out of there and didn't want to come back. But a strange thing happened. By Monday night several of those who had left came to know the Lord."

Gordy and his girl friend were among those who stormed away. Gordy's brother Lyle, who was a dedicated believer, was greatly concerned for him. On Monday night as soon as Lyle got home, he sought out Gordy.

"Why did you leave the way you did?" he asked bluntly. "What's the matter, couldn't you take it?"

Gordy was frank about the reason. He had been under such conviction that he had to leave or become a Christian. That night Lyle had the privilege of praying with his brother. But the miracle did not end there. Gordy's girl friend also received Christ, and so did the friend who left the retreat with them.

The following Sunday morning Evangelist Barry Moore was the speaker at the morning worship service in the church. That morning some of the others whose hearts were touched at the retreat made decisions.

"But that's not all," the Christian Education director continued. "I've had a procession of kids into my office since who have told me of decisions they made as the result of the retreat and the challenge Barry Moore brought."

Currently the Met has seventeen kids in Bible school, a number of whom are training for the ministry or the mission field. One of the present crop of Bible school graduates filled out an application form to go to northern Canada with the Northern Canada Evangelical Mission to work among the Indians. Others have taken part in various summer missionary programs, and there are those who are already serving in various capacities on mission fields around the world.

There are a number of good Bible camps around Ottawa but the camping program at the Met is admittedly weak. The regular church kids whose parents are concerned enough to send them get to go, but little is done for the underprivileged. The bus kids don't have the opportunity to go to camp.

Evangelism and outreach are important areas in the Metropolitan Bible Church ministry. Spearheaded by the strong Bible preaching of Pastor Herbert Arnold, it spreads out in many directions in an effort to help win Ottawa for Jesus Christ.

There is the music department and the TV and radio ministries which work so closely with it. There is the visitation program directed by Morry Worozbyt, laboring hand in hand with the Sunday school, the bus ministry and other activities which lend themselves to evangelism. There is the missionary program, and the Chinese Christian Fellowship which works with Chinese students across Canada.

In the case of the latter the church does nothing to direct the program. They allow the Chinese Christians to use the church building in their efforts to reach the Chinese young men and women who come to Ottawa to study. The group has their own program and their own leaders.

"The Chinese are so strongly family oriented," we were informed, "that they stay to themselves most of the time. But they have Bible studies and a great bunch of Christian young people."

Whether it was because he saw Orientals going into the building, or if God used some other means of bringing a young Korean to a service, we do not know. It doesn't really matter. He came, liked what he heard, and began to attend regularly.

That wasn't his only contact with the Christian religion, although he had been raised a Buddhist in Seoul. He came to Canada as a student and met a Korean girl (she was born in Philadelphia but had chosen Ottawa to go to college). It wasn't long until they were sharing an apartment, much to the dismay of the girl's devout Catholic mother.

In an effort to get them to be married the mother induced the young man to attend instruction classes with a view to joining the Catholic church. He went and tried to understand, but found it difficult. At the Met, however, he received Christ as his Saviour.

Worozbyt, in follow-up, gave him a copy of the book, *How To Be a Christian Without Being Religious*. He got convicted of the fact that it was sin for him to be living with his girl friend. They made plans to be married.

"He got her to come to church," Pastor Arnold related, "but she wasn't buying it. We became good friends, however, and he asked my wife and me to come over for a meal. But he tried to talk me out of witnessing to her. He kept telling me that she was so shy. The opportunity came and I did talk to her, but without results."

Then Barry Moore spoke and she went forward at the invitation following the morning service. The Saturday we were in Ottawa the young Korean couple was married.

"I think this wedding has thrilled me more than any other I've had since I've been in the ministry," Pastor Arnold said.

Morry Worozbyt told us of one of the visitation teams calling on a recent visitor after the man had been to church once.

"When I called to make an appointment for a team to talk with him and his wife, he was thrilled about it. 'I work with two fellows who go to your church,' he said. 'I've been watching them the last few months and they really are different. I'd like to have what they have.' "

Another principle for a thriving church was revealed. Those church members who worked with the new convert were *committed to Jesus Christ* and their lives measured up to their words.

The missionary emphasis at the Met is somewhat different than at most churches. They tried having a week of evening meetings, but attendance was spotty and the overall results were uncertain. So they started having a banquet for the young people on Thursday or Friday evening, using a missionary speaker. Saturday is devoted to a series of seminars, beginning quite early in the morning and continuing through the entire day. They have lunch and dinner in the church, so there is no need for anyone to leave.

"If we have four missionaries, each will set up his slide

projector and display his material in one of the rooms. The people will move from one place to the other seeing the pictures, listening to the story of the missionary's work and asking questions. It has worked out very well."

They have tried various methods of raising money for missions, including the faith-promise pledge. Nothing has worked as well, however, as letting people know what the need is and trusting God to bring the money in.

For many years the Met has been on the radio with good results. Recently they have been on television as well, with two different programs. One, which they buy time for, is televised over the station at Pembrooke, Ontario.

"Our goal," Pastor Arnold confided, "is to get on the Canadian Network. If we could make a network station in this area, we would have a potential audience of three million."

The other program, *Time to Live*, is on Cable Vision. It is a talk show and the time is furnished free. However, they had to invest $40,000 in equipment and train some of their own people to operate the cameras and the sound boards. They have children's stories, music, an interview with some outstanding Christian personality, and a Bible message on the hour-long program.

"The results have been encouraging," Pastor Arnold told us. "However, there is no doubt in my mind but that we do the morning service best. And we should. It's what we're trained to do."

The work of the Metropolitan Bible Church goes on, increasing in ever-widening circles as new activities and programs are added. It is another living proof that a downtown church need not wither and fade in effectiveness.

Even as we conducted the interviews at the Metropolitan Bible Church in Ottawa, we were sure Pastor Don Jost had correctly fingered the most important principle in the congregation's success. When the tapes were transcribed and we began to weigh the material, our convictions were strengthened. The unique plan of leadership was, indeed, the most important element in the growth of the church.

It was a type of leadership that required pastors who were strong on cooperation and without personal ambition to be in firm control and order others about, and it did work. We had seen it. And along with the leadership at the pastoral level, it incorporated a system that was most effective in developing a strong lay leadership.

6

Redwood Chapel Community Church, Castro Valley, California

One afternoon a few years ago Dr. Theodore Epp, founder of Back to the Bible Broadcast, Lincoln, Nebraska, and I were fishing on Dore Lake, Saskatchewan. The conversation drifted to the work of the Lord.

"I've always had the conviction that we are in error in the way we usually go about Christian effort," he said. "When man undertakes a project he appoints a committee and works out a big program, the bigger the better. But when God decides to do something, he chooses a man. Usually he selects someone with leadership qualities who has the vision to set lofty goals and the ability to get good men working harmoniously with him to get the job done."

So it was at the Redwood Chapel in Castro Valley, California. God called Sherman Williams from his responsibilities at Scripture Press to pastor the little independent church in one of San Francisco's more affluent suburbs. He had been closely associated with Sunday schools and churches in his work and was anxious to try certain principles he was sure God had helped him to develop.

We had already examined two fine churches with two radically different, but most productive, types of leadership. We were looking for still a third set of leadership qualities, a type that might be more adaptable to the situation of the average pastor serving the average church.

We found it in Sherman Williams. Frankly, however, he is so genial, so relaxed and unpreposing that at first we were not aware that our search had ended. He spoke of new ideas he had seen and developed during his years of visiting congregations around the country, and how anxious he was to put them into effect. He wanted to see if they would be of help to the Christian Church.

Although he accepted the invitation to Castro Valley, there were probably better places than this in California to try new ideas. The first pastor had been a man of great personal charisma and the congregation had known good growth while he led them. The church had been without a pastor for about six months. The group was only seven years old as a church, but the laymen were holding their own, looking for a man of God's choosing. They were meeting their bills with a budget of $53,000 yearly and an average Sunday morning attendance of 280.

Under Williams' capable leadership the congregation came alive. In two brief years attendance jumped to 392 and offerings climbed to $82,600. And by 1973, in spite of the fact that he firmly believed a church should not become larger than 500, the average Sunday morning crowd numbered 1,003, twice his ideal figure. The offerings were $300,000 and the missionary budget at $48,000 almost equalled their total income the year he moved to California. And by a comprehensive survey one-third of all the people in the area they could reasonably hope to reach had actually visited a service.

The gains in other avenues of the church are also impressive. The Sunday school now holds double sessions, Vacation Bible School has an attendance of more than 800 and discipleship classes for the more committed high schoolers and college and career kids are challenging them to full-time service for Jesus Christ.

An effective avenue of outreach has been discovered in cable television. Two years ago, the local cable system assigned to the Chapel the responsibility of programming one channel, 12b. A recent poll showed that more than half of the subscribers to cable TV in the area had watched at least one program. The telecasting of services and other programs from the church facility has encouraged those who are unable to attend and has provided an effective tool for teaching and evangelism in the Castro Valley area. The church also produced a half-hour variety program, "Sunday Nite Sing," which is aired on a number of other cable systems around the country.

Two satellite churches have been organized without visibly affecting the growth rate of the mother church. In 1968 a new work in Pleasanton was started. With the blessing and encouragement of the pastor and the board, 70 regular members of the Chapel transferred their allegiance and support to the new work. Today more than 200 are worshipping there with regularity and all phases of the ministry are growing.

In 1973 a second new church was launched at Fremont, California. Again a group left Redwood Chapel to give the new effort stability and financial strength. Meetings were begun on Sunday in October of 1973, and when we visited Castro Valley early in 1974 more than 100 were in the service on the average Sunday morning. Souls were coming to Christ and an aura of excitement and anticipation prevaded the new work.

"And still we're bursting at the seams," Rev. Neal Doty, the associate pastor, told us. "our long range goals look to organizing several new churches in places our surveys have shown a strong gospel witness is needed."

Pastor Williams, or Sherm as he is known to the staff and his close friends, is still concerned about the size of Redwood Chapel.

"I still haven't changed my conviction that no church should have more people in it than the number the pastor can get to know personally. I see the responsibility of the church as reaching beyond evangelism, as important as that is, to deal with the whole person. It isn't enough to lead a man to Christ, pat him on the back and tell him to go out and live the way he should and reach others for Christ. We've got to help our new converts get grounded in the Word and so solidly established in their faith that they will become what Jesus Christ wants them to be."

I couldn't help commenting. "It seems that God has different ideas than you do about the size Redwood Chapel ought to be."

"I have thought about that, too. Believe me. We certainly aren't going to limit our activities for Him, or stop reaching out to unbelievers in an effort to keep the church the size I want it. If God continues to give us more people, I'm not going to argue with Him. We'll just work as best we can and forget about numbers."

The size of the congregation and its continued growth has created problems for Pastor Williams. He could allow his own philosophy about the ideal size of a church to be pushed aside and allow the Chapel to grow as much as it would. Some of the larger churches he had visited retained the warmth and friendliness of a country church. Others became cold and impersonal, a gigantic, well-oiled machine that ground out x number of programs every week like a computor sorting figures.

But he didn't want to risk that. He was even more deeply convinced that God wanted the church family to be just that. The fellowship of believers was to be the same as that in the dedicated Christian family where there is concern about the heartaches and sorrows of each other and rejoicing at each victory. Although the terminology he uses is different from that of Dr. W. A. Criswell at First Baptist Church in Dallas, the solution is substantially the same.

"We must have a total church program," he went on. "It's our goal, regardless of the number of people who call Redwood Chapel their church home, to build a well-rounded program that will minister across age, educational and interest lines."

Dr. Criswell says, "Regardless of the size of the church, it must have something for everybody."

According to associate pastor Neal Doty this is the reason the church has such a strong music department and Sunday school and youth work.

"Actually," he told us, "we have a balanced program. I doubt that any of us could point to a certain phase of our ministry as the reason for the Chapel's success. I don't mean to be critical of them but, as an example, some churches can point to a fleet of buses or an aggressive visitation campaign as the reason for their success. We can't do that. Each staff member is encouraged to give his very best to his responsibilities, as though theirs is the most important in our entire ministry. You'd be surprised at how important that encouragement is in the morale of our staff."

Rev. Williams mentioned another conviction of his that has played an important part in shaping the personality of the church.

"Some times we pastors have a tendency to look only at the way a given program may affect our own little sphere. Young Life comes along, for example, and immediately we ask ourselves, 'Is this program going to pull the loyalty of some of our kids from the church?' A couple gets involved in a prison ministry or the Gideons and we are concerned that they may be missing a few services or giving a little money to a cause other than our own.

"I firmly believe that we have to look at the ministry of Jesus Christ as a whole and judge a work by its outreach and effectiveness. We encourage our people to take part in other activities that truly exalt Christ. As a result we have had at least half of the Young Life staff members in our area worshipping with us. I'm sure our philosophy has helped in developing a strong missionary interest and concern for the unsaved within our church."

Probably no area is subject to wider interpretation than that of effective leadership. Pastor Williams has a different concept than those who believe that God has ordained him to lead the flock and the people should have little to say about what is done. He has a hand in the shaping of policy, and many, if not most, of the programs originate first out of his own concern for the people. But his is a gentle touch. He acquaints the board and the congregation with the needs he would like to see the church meet, gives them time to understand his concern and proposals and when decisions are made, they are the decisions of the people.

"I'll never forget my early months here," Joseph Linn, director of music, told us. "I was still in college when I got acquainted with the Chapel almost ten years ago. I got acquainted with Pastor Williams' daughter, Sharon (now Mrs. Martin Erickson), when we worked together in Youth for Christ.

"When I came here to direct music I had a lot to learn. One of the first times I met with Pastor Williams I gave him a lengthy discourse on the guitar as an instrument, what it could do musically, and why I wanted to use it in the services. He was most gracious. I didn't find out until months later that he knew more about the guitar than I would ever know.

"At first I went to him and cleared the things I wanted to do in the way of music for the church. I was young and inexperienced and needed direction. But as I gained in knowledge and began to understand how things should be done, I gradually assumed more and more responsibility. He didn't make a big thing of it. I was hardly aware that I was reaching the place where I was on my own more than before. I can see now that the pastor was watching me closely as he trained me to take over the music of the church without his supervision.

"He knows what's going on in the Music Department. He know's what's being done in each area and if he felt we weren't effective we'd hear about it. But when he gives us a job he also gives us the responsibility and authority we need to carry it out."

Neal Doty, the associate pastor, agreed with what the director of music said and added a few comments of his own.

"I've been familiar with other multiple staffed churches," he said, "and have seen all sorts of senior pastors. Some of those who are the most authoritarian are basically afraid of their staffs and are insecure. There are those who never allow one of their men to appear in the pulpit. Others do so infrequently and their people never really learn whether one of the staff can speak effectively or not.

"At present I'm preaching four times a month. Twice at the new work at Fremont and twice here. Pastor Williams is relaxed and secure in the knowledge that he is not going to be eclipsed by one of his people when it comes to preaching. I know he rejoices when one of us does well.

"There's complete harmony among our staff. I think this is one of the reasons."

When Pastor Sherman Williams came to Castro Valley in 1961, the church was small but solidly established. By most standards it would have been considered a good church.

As soon as their furniture was in the house, the dishes unpacked and the inevitable reception was over, Rev. Williams asked representatives of the various boards to meet with him every Monday night. The first item on the agenda was a discussion of their goals.

"What is our reason for existence?" he wanted to know. "What do we want to accomplish?"

The easy answers came quickly. But as they discussed the matter they realized establishing goals was not easy to do. Stripped of evangelical jargon, their own concepts needed focus.

A little effort could plan a program that would have something at church three or four nights a week. But what did a policy like that do for the individual? What effect was it having on his spiritual life? And what about his family? Was he able to spend any time with his kids during those early, formative years?

"I have a strong conviction," Pastor Williams said, "that the church is made for the people. We can't fill a man's time with working for God, regardless of his competence, at the expense of feeding him spiritually. If we do, there is a danger that he will grow cold and indifferent to Jesus Christ and limit, or destroy, his effectiveness.

"I'm also satisfied that not taking any part in the ministry of the local church can be deadening. If a man or woman continually sits in services soaking in the Word but never using it, he is going to soak and sour. Either extreme renders him useless.

"For that reason we encourage each believer to discover and develop his or her own spiritual gifts."

As the discussions continued goals emerged.

"There is no better place to learn what the church should be than to look at it through the Scriptures," the minister went on. "We studied the elements that made up the early church as described in the book of Acts. First there is doctrine. The people had to learn what they believed and why. Then there was teaching. Converts had to be instructed in Christian living and how to share Jesus Christ with those who don't know Him. There was the concept of worship, fellowship, communion, and witnessing. Basically those represented the spiritual goals we wanted to establish."

In evangelism they wanted to win a man to Christ, train him and encourage him to develop his Christian life to maturity so he could reproduce himself by winning others.

Once those broad goals were set down they moved to a different area, still somewhat generalized but not specific as to implementation. They had to decide what the thrust of their congregation would be. What did they hope to accomplish?

Theirs was to be a *family oriented church*. They were all agreed on that. Family was to be the key for worship. That meant they would not only have to meet the needs of the youth and adults; they would also have to develop a means of helping each child to learn to worship at the level of his understanding.

They wanted Redwood Chapel to be a church of *fellowship rooted in the Word*. They wanted the people to learn to know and love each other, to encourage each other in their faith.

They were concerned about providing *adequate teaching of the Scriptures for all ages*. Knowing the Bible is the key to successful Christian living and has to be the basis for every effective church, they determined to encourage, even the adults, to learn more of its teaching.

Training and the developing of leadership had to have a prominent place in the activities of the church. They were as concerned about involving the primary kids in the active participation so vital in the developing of leadership as they were the senior high and college and career groups and the adults.

"We wanted our people to be able to read Scripture or speak or pray in public without embarrassment," one of the men explained. "That meant they would have to be trained, especially while they were young."

° ° °

No one had ever set down the goal of the Music Department in simple words. Now they knew, specifically, what they wanted to accomplish. *It should be a means of worship and outreach for all ages.* It wasn't enough to have a choir because most churches have one. Nor could they be content to select those whose natural talents made for better music. The spiritual discernment of the people who were singing had to be determined.

"The church insisted that the Music Department have a vital role in the worship service," Linn, the director of music, told us. "They wanted those who sang to do so as a ministry to God."

Their goals included a strong emphasis on the youth of the congregation and the community. *The young people had to be kept involved in Sunday school meetings and week-day activities.*

Last, they wanted outreach to be an integral part of both the church and the congregation. The Chapel had always been somewhat concerned about missions. Now they wanted to greatly increase the scope of their interest, including efforts of their own, as well as the activities of established home and foreign missions.

But they did not want their interest to stop there. They wanted to train their people in sharing their faith and to encourage them to do so, both in organized church efforts such as regular visitation and personal witnessing at work and in their homes.

Once those goals were defined and set down on paper they were ready to survey what they were doing in each area. They had to decide what was going on and how it related to the total program.

"We wanted to develop a total ministry." Pastor Williams emphasized again. "So we made a chart that would show us if we were emphasizing evangelism at the expense of worship, for example, or if we were heavy on fellowship and lacking in a zeal for souls. It was a revealing survey. In many ways I was surprised, and I was not alone. I'm sure that some on the committee were shocked at our findings."

The survey focused attention on the Sunday school. Almost everyone in the church thought it was doing a satisfactory job. Now they realized it could be made much more effective, and would have to be if it was to assume its rightful place in the total program of the church.

The Sunday school was basic in Rev. Williams' plans. It provided the Christian education program, the sturdy foundation that would provide a continuing supply of workers and church leaders. The Sunday school involved a lot of people. It made it possible for the pastor to multiply himself many times over by training teachers and getting them to help him in the work of the Lord.

The problem in the Sunday school of Redwood Chapel was the same as that in many Sunday schools around the country. There was a lack of well-trained teachers.

"There was lots of activity," the pastor said, "but we didn't have any definable goals, so there was no way of regularly measuring what we were doing."

The pastor knew what was wrong and was sure he had the answer, but he did not want to run ahead of the people. He discussed the matter with them and they began to talk it over among themselves. His ideas became their ideas and it wasn't long until they were ready to act.

A survey of the interests, educational qualifications and abilities of each member of the congregation was made. Job descriptions were developed for departmental superintendents and teachers. Training classes were established and a policy of teacher evaluation and limited appointments was worked out. (All teachers are appointed for a term of one year. Lacking reappointment, they are through at the end of that period.)

As a part of changing their Sunday school they entered a national Sunday School Association contest and won the grand prize in 1967. It was the only contest they ever entered.

"I've never been too keen on contests," Pastor Williams informed us, "but it provided the incentive we needed to work more rapidly than we might have done otherwise."

Winston Miller, the Christian Education director, was also with Scripture Press before coming to Castro Valley. He had been responsible for holding workshops in churches all over the country and had been active in Sunday school conventions.

"I picked up a lot of ideas during those years," he said, "that have proved helpful in our situation here. For example, we grade our children up through the junior high department, giving them a report card every quarter. Those with a grade of 90 or above get a gold seal on their cards and are placed on our honor roll."

Youth director Donald Larmour also runs a balanced program, walking the narrow path between excitement and recreation on one side and serious Bible study and discipleship classes on the other.

"Actually," he told us, "both are important. We are as concerned about running a well-rounded program as any department of the church. Kids need a wholesome outlet for their boundless energy and a place where they can make the right kind of friends.

"It is also imperative that they are thoroughly grounded in the Scriptures and that those with leadership abilities are challenged to special dedication."

At the time we were there they had a discipleship group for college men, taught by the director of the youth department, and two others for high school students. The group for the older guys meets at six in the morning.

"I'm glad to see that," the youth director went on. "A guy's got to mean business with God to get up in time to get to *any* Christian meeting at that hour."

The recreational activities of the Youth Department have been a means of reaching many who were outside the church and ignorant or indifferent to the claims of Jesus Christ on their lives.

"That's the kind of a guy I was when I first went to one of the Halloween parties," a fine young Christian by the name of Rick Reed told us. "It was my first contact with Redwood Chapel in 1970. They had this spook house set up at the Masonic Temple and it was really neat. I saw a lot of kids from my own high school so I felt at home.

"It was like everyone else in the room had disappeared when the speaker was talking. It was just between God and me. About 50 kids made decisions for Christ that night. . . . I have worked in several Halloween parties since I graduated from high school and went on to college. I'm kind of sold on that method of getting the kids in."

There were 350 kids at the Halloween party where Rick made his decision for Christ. The speaker of the evening was so surprised to see 50 hands go up that he was sure his listeners must have misunderstood him. He went back and explained once more what it meant to become a Christian.

When he finished he told them he wanted only those who really meant it to stand and walk out the back door.

"Those kids had to fight their way over the bodies of other kids sprawled all over the place to get to the back door," Doty went on. "But all 50 did it. One of them (Rick Reed) eventually became president of our youth group."

Ten of that number associated themselves with the Redwood Chapel. The others had connections with other churches in the vicinity.

In 1973 the senior high Halloween party was attended by 450. The junior high party the following night was somewhat smaller.

Traditionally, the Halloween parties are the starting point for a brief annual evangelistic thrust. The speaker for the special meetings, which run from Sunday through Wednesday nights, is also the speaker for the kids.

"It works out very well," one of the staff informed us. "The kids who respond initially are taken a few steps further along the Christian life while everything is new and interesting to them."

From the beginning of his ministry at Redwood Chapel, Pastor Williams had emphasized the desirability of getting into the area of using broadcast tools to communicate gospel truth. The church went on the radio with the "Sunday Nite Sing" in the fall of 1963, just four years after Williams arrived. Through the years the congregation was kept apprised of the developments in the radio and TV field. When cable television became a reality, the church was ready to move out in faith and pioneered the programming of a cable TV channel. Purchasing equipment and building to accommodate TV production, the church caught the attention of the local cable system, which offered the use of a channel. Now, 24 hours each day, good gospel music and good news of salvation is fed to more than 5,000 homes in the area.

"When we were offered the opportunity to have a TV channel, we didn't lose any time getting into the act," Doty said. "We weren't exactly sure what we were getting into, but we knew the influence TV could have on lives and we wanted a slice of it for God."

They began by televising their services. People thought they must have changed the format when they went on TV, sharpening the singing and streamlining the program to make it more interesting for home viewing. Actually, all they did was add some lights.

"I think you would have to say the camera is like a spectator in the audience," the associate minister explained, "seeing what goes on. In our other programming the camera becomes a creative tool to be used by the producer."

The "Sunday Nite Sing," a half-hour program produced for television, could best be described as a variety show. They have a fifteen-piece orchestra, assembled and directed by Joe Linn, that does the opening theme. There is an eight-voice ensemble that sings, and usually there will be a guest on the program. It has been well received locally and is beginning to attract attention in other parts of the country. They are now on three radio stations and seven or eight cable systems.

"We could add a lot more," Mr. Doty volunteered. "I have a stack of letters here on my desk asking about it. I take my time answering them because we don't want to add more outlets than we can take care of. We're putting one new cable system on now."

They have some programming for children but most of it is for adults.

"We try to put some life and fun into our efforts," Mr. Doty went on. "So many of the Christian telecasts I see are hand-holding programs. You get the impression they are sitting at your bedside trying to find some word of solace before you gasp your last breath. We want to present a life with Jesus Christ as vibrant and joyous."

Linn and Doty try to have an acceptable balance in the music that is presented. To be contemporary without being offensive is not the easiest thing to do.

Not long ago a young man from Kansas City came in and handed Joe Linn an arrangement of a new song. It wasn't printed. In fact, it looked as though he had made a few chicken scratches on paper as he waited for a light to change. The music director had copies xeroxed, passed them out to the band and they ran through it. It was an upbeat song titled, "Get All Excited."

"Get all excited," the first line urged; "go tell everybody that Jesus Christ is King."

They used it but with some misgivings. They liked it and the musicians liked it, but they wondered about some of the older, more staid listeners in the community.

The answer wasn't long in coming. An elderly woman called from a nursing home in San Jose. She was so thrilled with the song she wanted a tape of it so she could play it when she was able to save enough money to get a tape recorder.

There isn't a great deal of mail that comes in from the TV programs. The response is usually by word of mouth, but there was mail on that song—all of it favorable.

The television channel is an important arm of the church but not all important. It takes its place in the total program of Redwood Chapel. This is the secret of the church and Pastor Sherman Williams' leadership.

When we finished our work in Castro Valley we had examined three types of leadership. The first was that of Dr. W. A. Criswell, senior pastor at First Baptist Church in Dallas. The second was the unusual group leadership by both pastors and laymen at Metropolitan Bible Church in Ottawa. Now we had studied the leadership of Pastor Sherman Williams, a gentle, relaxed leadership that inspired and guided towards well-defined goals, but was so low profile few realized its forcefulness.

"I think we're ready to make an addition to our list of principles for building an effective church," I said as we waited for a cab to take us back to our motel.

1. ANALYSIS AND EVALUATION
2. STRONG BIBLE EMPHASIS
3. LOVE
4. DYNAMIC LEADERSHIP

10

Northwest Bible Church, Fort Worth, Texas

By the time we reached Forth Worth and headed for the Northwest Bible Church, we had a general idea of what we were looking for. Most of our formula for a vigorous, growing church was on paper, a neat list of the qualities we had discovered and verified in other groups. The rest was taking shape in our minds, waiting only to be expanded and examined through the experiences of other congregations.

We needed churches that would help us to prove the principle that a church must be adaptable to the needs of its people. We had found that element in First Baptist Church in Dallas, First Alliance in Mansfield, and in the Johnston Heights Free Church in Surey, British Columbia; but there had been other, more significant factors in all of those churches.

"We're sure it's true," Marge said, "but we need churches that zero in on it."

I nodded.

"We've got to find a church that's like a rifle with a 6-power scope when it comes to meeting the needs of the people."

Going directly to Fort Worth's Northwest Bible Church from the huge First Baptist in Dallas proved to be an unnerving experience. Our thinking was attuned to an 18,000 membership, a four-block building complex in the heart of the city and a budget of five million dollars a year and growing.

It was not that the independent Fort Worth church was so modest in size. Actually it was a flourishing work with an average attendance of 450 to 475 at two Sunday morning services, and they had five buses and a growing Sunday school.

Attendance and membership were increasing at the comfortable rate of 15% each year, a percentage considerably higher than the growth rate of the three communities it bordered.

Hiding as it was along the busy thoroughfare, we drove past the simple, unpretentious building without even noticing it, although we had the correct address and a good map. Some twenty minutes and three stops for directions later, we found someone who could tell us how to get to the church. Retracing our route, we finally located it half a mile south of where we were.

We soon discovered that the Fort Worth congregation met our requirements exactly. A comparatively new group, organized in 1962, it had adapted so well to the needs of the people around it that it had grown steadily from the very beginning. Most of the gain was in young families who came in by conversion, or those who had wearied of liberal preaching and transferred to the Bible church where they could hear solid gospel messages.

The pastor, Dr. Leslie Madison, was called to Fort Worth after completing his doctrinal studies at Dallas Theological Seminary and ministered to the group of 80 that was meeting in the Lions Club. Formerly the people had been members of an evangelical congregation within a liberal denomination. When difficulties developed they were locked out of their building. The embryo congregation could not be considered a group of young people at the time, even by their own designation. There was too much white hair among them.

"If I remember correctly," Dr. Madison said, "fifty-five of the original eighty were within five years of retirement or older. They were a tremendous group of believers, mature and dedicated. No one could accuse them of rash, hot-headed action. Yet, their very age seemed to stand in the way of the growth of the new work. And few pastors would deliberately choose a nucleus of older believers to start a new congregation. Most of us have equated building with the young."

But the original group were not content to have it stay that way. They were determined to reach out to the unsaved young couples of Fort Worth. With that in mind they deliberately chose to work among the younger married couples. They attracted those who were above average in education, leadership and income.

In order to become a youthful church the program had to be changed. It had to have a strong Sunday school and a strong family orientation.

The church could have become a nice, comfortable place for the retired to worship had the people not been adaptable. They knew a change was required and set about to do what was necessary to make their program attractive to the people they wanted to reach. As a result they have been able to have an effective ministry with younger families, many of whom have small children.

'Chief' Jones was one of those. His was the first black family to call the Northwest Bible Church their own.

"I'll never forget when he came in with his wife and children," Dr. Madison told us, leaning back in his chair and cupping his hands behind his head. "They were well dressed and refined and were looking for a place where the gospel was preached. When the morning worship service was over they were warmly received.

'Chief' Jones, as everyone called him, had received Christ at a Christian Servicemen's Center while stationed overseas. He was back in Texas now, serving out his last hitch before retirement.

The Sunday before we were there a nice looking girl with blond hair and blue eyes came in and wanted to know if 'Chief' Jones had come in yet.

"I was a bit surprised," the pastor informed us, "as I pointed him out to her."

"My daddy works for him out at Carswell (Air Force Base)," she explained. "The 'Chief's' been telling me so much about your church and how I should come here that I've finally decided to see what it's like. I want to sit with him and his family."

There are a number of 'Chief' Jones in the congregation, who are concerned about presenting Jesus Christ to those they work with. They were not content to see the church rest on the gains of the past.

The church is situated at a place where three different suburbs come together. Strangely, each represents a different strata of society. One is made up largely of people with low incomes who have moved there because of lower taxes and inexpensive property. The second consists of nice homes and spacious yards. Those who live there have considerably higher incomes than the average. They are young executives and professional types who are on the way up. The third furnishes a place to live for those who have already arrived. They are men who have climbed the ladder to a comfortable height. The incomes of most are large and they can, and many do, travel in expensive circles.

But there is one thing in common among all three groups. The Lord Jesus Christ has wiped out their other differences and made them equal.

"When we were building our church it wasn't uncommon to have a bank executive carrying mortar to a common laborer who knew how to lay blocks," the pastor said.

Because of the difference in the incomes and social standings of those from the more affluent suburbs, however, few from Samson Park would attend the church—or if they did visit, they would only come once or twice. It seemed to disturb them that the others had so much more money than they did.

"And it isn't because of any superior attitude on the part of the more affluent. That I can assure you."

The resentment and barrier came from those who were not so fortunate. The men from the other suburbs did everything they could to make the less well-to-do feel comfortable. They wore mis-matched trousers and jackets to church and a couple of them tried coming in jeans. Their wives left their expensive clothes hanging in the closet so their dresses would more nearly match those of the Samson Park people. If they had second cars, they drove them, so their expensive new cars would not be prominent in the church parking lot. They were trying, as best they could, to 'adapt' to the families of the older suburb.

Whether the ones they were trying to reach felt inferior or knew of the 'dressing down' and considered it condescending, or if they simply did not enjoy the company of those so far removed from themselves on the social and economic scale we do not know. The fact remains that the people of the church were quite willing to make personal changes if they would have an opportunity to minister to the other group.

When a survey showed that Samson Park was a fertile field for a bus ministry, the church bought two vehicles. The survey showed that the area was made up largely of low income families with little or no church background, and that parents would be glad to see their children go to Sunday school if someone picked them up and brought them home.

The congregation could have turned away from trying to reach that area after being rebuffed on their first effort. But they didn't. They began to operate buses in that area and now have five buses with routes three miles or less from the church. They also have an active, aggressive 'Good News' program (Child Evangelism) and a strong visitation plan. They are working hard to strike a responsive chord in the hearts of the people of Samson Park. Although their efforts to reach adults has been largely unproductive, they are vigorous in their efforts to reach the kids.

Although there is a constant effort to make the church program meet the needs of the people they are reaching or want to reach, there are comparatively few innovations that differ radically from traditional methods.

"I'm not one who believes we have to throw out everything that has been done in the past in order to meet the needs of the hearts of our people," Dr. Madison said. "Sin is still sin and the problems people face as the result of it are no different now than they were 20 years ago. The answer is still the same—Jesus Christ. This is what I keep telling our people."

Their communion service, which formerly was a part of the morning service once each quarter is now held at night, and they usually have testimonies and a time of sharing.

"That and the overhead projector I use on Sunday night as a Bible-teaching aid are about the extent of our changes at present," he went on. "I have found that our people want an order of worship they are familiar with. We make changes. We're not locked in to any particular form, but we usually leave the service the same for at least a year."

He paused, seriously, and when he began to speak again the subject changed.

"I think I told you that we have a young and affluent congregation. Many of our most active couples are professional men or executives with important responsibilities. Do you want to know what has attracted them to us? It isn't some fancy program or spell-binding messages.

"It's the Word of God. Our emphasis is on Bible teaching, as simply and straightforward as it is possible to make it.

I would say we adapt more to the needs of our people in this way than in any other. This is what our entire congregation needs—perhaps more so than others. Many of our people have little or no background in the Word of God. If they are going to be challenged for Christ and grow spiritually, they have to be fed on the Scriptures."

Because a large percentage are comparatively young and have small families, Rev. Madison has urged them to enroll in the Basic Youth Conflict seminars. At the time we conducted our interviews more than 100 couples from the Northwest Bible Church had taken part in at least one of the Gothard series of meetings.

"We've seen some exciting changes take place in the lives of some of our people," he continued. "There's no way of estimating what they have accomplished. And, basically, they are simply biblical principles applied to everyday life."

Occasionally, during the training hour, Mrs. Madison teaches a group of women in a Notebook Seminar on such subjects as "How to Be a Successful Wife and Mother." Dr. Madison has the men, teaching a course on "How to Be the Spiritual Leader in the Home."

"Although these training sessions are inspired by Gothard's program and in some way are patterned after it, they amount to Bible training," he went on. "We take the seven basic principles Gothard sets forth and teach the people how to use them in their day-to-day associations with their families and with others."

He went on to say he has been surprised at how little most unbelievers actually know about the Word of God. Even in the South, which is the Bible Belt of the country, there is an astonishing ignorance of the Scriptures.

Bible studies had long been an integral part of the lives of the more devout members of the congregation, but now they saw the need of organizing them and having studies that would reach the most people for Christ.

When they began to develop a Bible study program for the purpose of outreach, they chose a study book so elementary the pastor described it as being almost childish in its approach.

"It is the Bible Walk-Through Program," he explained. "It gives a quick, bird's-eye view of the Bible in thirteen lessons. One part of the living room will be Egypt, another Cana, and so on. The teacher has the students walk through the countries involved in the history and migrations of the children of Israel, and those Paul visited on his missionary journeys. It sounds silly, but it's surprising how effective a study like that is in helping those who aren't acquainted with the Word to understand it."

As far as we were concerned it was more evidence of the adaptability of the congregation and the pastor. They wanted a course of study to help challenge the non-Christian and to help the new believer who has had no Bible background. A course as simple as second grade spelling is called for.

When we were in Fort Worth in 1974 there were four or five such studies in operation and the goal was for fifteen before the year was half out. Ken Honrock, the assistant pastor, was holding training classes for interested members of the congregation so they could be more effective in leading similar groups.

Several women have come to Christ as the result of the women's Bible studies, and at least two families are now regular in church attendance because of the evening studies for couples.

The Word of God takes an important place in the Sunday school curriculum, the youth work, and in every department of the church. It is the cornerstone on which the Northwest Bible Church is based.

The second prerequisite for a thriving church is also present. The people have a deep, abiding love for each other and for those outside the church. We saw evidence of it everywhere.

"I guess I first became aware of the depth of the love people have for each other when I saw them working on the addition to our church," Dr. Madison informed us.

o   o   o

In 1970, after a year of operation, the buses brought in more kids than the facilities could take care of. The congregation was faced with a dilemma. They could go into an expansion program they lacked the funds for, or they could retreat to a more modest plan of outreach and growth.

We were reminded of something a Canadian pastor friend told us. "Remember, the chickens will always die off to adjust the size of the flock to the size of the coop."

During the discussion one of the men suggested that they build the addition themselves.

"We can't go into a full-fledged building program with the amount of money we could reasonably expect to come in. But we could scrape up enough to pay for the material if we do the work ourselves. We certainly don't want to have to tell the kids we can't send the buses out for them anymore, that we don't have room for them."

With minimum of discussion the motion passed by an overwhelming majority.

"I wasn't sure just how that would work out," the pastor continued. "We didn't have many blue collar workers in our church. I didn't know how much work those velvet-soft hands of young professional and managerial people could do. We soon found out."

They took out the back wall of the nave, raised the building high enough to put in a steel beam to bear the load formerly carried by the wall they removed.

"A lot of folks said that it couldn't be done, but we had an engineer in the church who said it could and he directed the project.

"The money the church saved on labor made the difference between our being able to do the building at the time we really needed it, or having to wait for more affluent days," the pastor continued. "The rest was unseen. A depth of fellowship and love developed among those who worked together on the building that I would not have believed possible."

Then he said something we had often heard other pastors say. "I would strongly recommend to any church that it do some of the construction work themselves, regardless of the financial condition of the congregation. I think it did more than all the sermons on love I could have ever preached."

Things have happened since that building project to give the people opportunity to express their love for others in ways far more effective than in words.

For some reason the church has had more difficulty in attracting those in the lower income bracket than others who were more affluent. A Latin American family which lived in nearby Samson Park, however, was a notable exception. They loved each other and the more distant members of their family so much it was a lesson in Christian love to the rest of the congregation. In the end it resulted in the people having an opportunity to show the shy, dark family their appreciation and love for them.

The father and mother, gray before their time, not only took care of their own children, they had five other nieces staying with them, three of whom were from Old Mexico.

"But no one ever heard the man complain," we were told. "Working as hard as he had to work to feed so many must have been discouraging for him but he didn't show it. Neither did he reveal any resentment at having to shoulder such a burden."

Three or four months after they started to attend the church, the husband and wife and all the kids received Jesus Christ. Because the girls were so hesitant and uncomfortable in the regular service, a Junior High Church was organized. Within their own age group they felt a little more free and relaxed.

Then the father died suddenly.

When the people heard about it the entire congregation was crushed. He had social security, of course, but funds were only provided through that source for his legal heirs. The others he had been caring for could expect no social security payments.

"So the church undertook to help them," Dr. Madison related. "It was our way of saying 'thank you' to a wonderful family.

"We learned something from that experience. I think it taught us that when one of His children are sorrowing or in need, we are all affected by it."

For a number of years the Bible Church has had close contact with the Child Evangelism workers in the Dallas-Fort Worth area. It has become their greatest evangelical outreach, both in lives touched for Christ and in the increased dedication and commitment on the part of those involved. That is especially true in the lives of teenagers who have helped with the teaching of Five Day clubs. In 1973, 40 women in the church had 25 clubs, resulting in more than 500 professions of faith.

In a different phase of the ministry the church helped operate the Good News Bus in one of the booths at the Stock Show and Rodeo held in the Will Rogers Colliseum every year. People, and especially kids, went in the front door, through the bus and out the back door. When they left they had learned about heaven and how to get there. The entire program took twenty minutes and was constantly repeated. Many teenagers, carefully trained, worked in the bus. It provided a terrific challenge for them.

In 1973, 2700 children went through the bus in one week's time. There were more than 700 professions of faith. Many of that number went into the follow-up program, but the figures were unavailable.

The Good News clubs range in numbers of kids from a dozen to 40 with an overall average of 25. At least 400 are involved in all the clubs every week.

"In a way," Dr. Madison said, "we have a larger Sunday school during the week than we have on Sunday."

The Five Day clubs are teen-oriented insofar as teachers are concerned and are set up for the summer months. Those who are interested in the program go through ten days of special training in dealing with children. Then they go out to put into practice what they have been taught.

They will go to the backyard of an interested person who may, or may not, be a believer, or they'll take a bus to an area where there are plenty of kids. Then they will go out with printed handbills or fliers inviting the kids in to the Daily Vacation Bible School they will be holding. It's not difficult to get out the kids. They love the program.

The teaching team (there are three involved with each club) divides the responsibilities. One will lead the singing, one tells the missionary story, and the other tells the Bible story. The program takes an hour and a half each day for five days in one location.

In 1973, 15 kids were teaching with from 400 to 500 children attending. Many are from racial minorities and a large percentage have had little or no contact with the gospel of Jesus Christ.

"One girl who received Christ during the Five Day club program in the summer of '73 came into my office last week," the pastor told us. "One of the boys on the teaching team had spent five hours talking with her one afternoon before she was able to understand what it meant to become a believer. . . . She has been baptized herself and is now praying that her entire family will be saved.

"I think I'm more thrilled by the spiritual growth of the teaching corps," Dr. Madison went on, "than I am about the numbers reached for Christ. I'm convinced those fifteen kids who were teaching last year are going to be soul winners all their lives. You can't imagine how excited they are."

One of their number taught for the first time the year before. The next summer he turned down a good job because taking it would have meant that he would not be able to go out and work with the Five Day clubs.

"I just can't do it, Pastor," he said. "I've *got* to go out and work with those kids."

The Five Day clubs, with the policy of using teen teachers, play an important role in helping that segment of the congregation to commit themselves totally to Jesus Christ. It is but another example of the way in which the church has met the needs of their people. Growth comes by serving and work. They are putting their youth to work.

Dr. Madison feels the key to any success the Northwest Bible Church may have had is directly related to the emphasis that is placed on the Word of God. Our research agreed with his appraisal, but we had found a factor that was also most important. The pastor and the board had sensed the needs of the people and had enough love and concern for them to attempt to meet those needs.

Many of the methods were staid and traditional, but knowing the makeup and background of the congregation, the people needed exactly that sort of programming. Other methods were changed or added to the total picture as the need was evidenced. There were many good examples of that procedure, like the Child Evangelism Five Day clubs and the Walk-Through Bible studies that were attracting so much interest from the people in the vicinity. There were also the Bill Gothard seminars which the people had been encouraged to attend to help them with their family and personal relationships.

We knew, now, that ADAPTABILITY did belong on our list of principles for an effective church, but we had one other series of interviews in that area to be completed, although we were not even aware of them yet.

11

Lakewood Evangelical Free Church, White Bear Lake, Minnesota

Leaving Fort Worth to fly to Chicago for a series of board meetings, we thought we had only one more principle to verify. And we would soon be going to San Francisco to complete that. When we got to Oak Park, the suburb of Chicago where one of our board meetings was to be held, we were intrigued by the story we heard of another church. Our good friend and fellow board member, Dr. Harold Broman, invited us to visit his church.

"It's small, but we're all excited about it," he told us, when he learned of the project we were working on. "We were organized as an outreach ministry by the First Free Church of St. Paul (Minnesota) a few years ago. Now we're completely self-supporting. We have a new building and are about crowded out of it. Our people are involved in Bible studies all over the place. And some of them, including our pastor, have been in on the astonishing things that have happened at St. Peters' Catholic Church in North St. Paul."

Rev. Donald Leigh and most of the people in the congregation, he went on, had an entirely different idea of what the church and its facilities should be.

"We decided to go back to the Scriptures and learn for ourselves exactly what the early church was and what it should be for us."

Believers in the early church had a sense of fellowship and community. They loved each other and were concerned when sorrow or troubles came to one of their number. When one person was hurting they all hurt with him, holding him up with love and prayer.

And they met wherever they could. They gave little thought to bricks and mortar because of a strong conviction that the church is people.

"We realized we had to have a building to meet in," we were told, "and we wanted it to be a church home. Something that would not be an affront to visitors and to the new believers we were praying would come in. But we didn't want to spend the Lord's money on a traditional building. We instructed our architect to come up with a design consisting of several multi-purpose rooms."

Even the nave in their new structure was designed so it could be used for other meetings than the regular worship services. The pastor stood on the same level as the people were sitting, using a portable, free-standing pulpit that could be moved with ease. They had stacks of folding chairs to take the place of pews, so they could be shifted around, or taken out if the situation called for that. The kitchen opened off the sanctuary.

"One couple came all the way across town to attend our services," the pastor laughed. "We asked them why they drove by so many other churches to come to ours.

" 'We drove by this church one Sunday and were intrigued by it. We decided we had to come and see what kind of people would put up such a peculiar looking church.' "

"Our church is adaptable, too," Harold concluded. "In fact, I would say that 'adaptability' is probably the key to our entire program, but we're adaptable in a different way than I've ever seen before."

We were interested in the church at White Bear Lake. It sounded as though it might add a new dimension to this portion of the book. Yet we couldn't hop a plane and look at every church that was suggested to us. So we did some checking with knowledgeable friends in the Twin City area. Our new contacts verified Harold's appraisal.

The Minnesota church was different. It was as sound scripturally and as thoroughly evangelical as the Fort Worth congregation, but its entire approach was different.

We made plans to go to the Twin Cities as soon as we

could work it into our schedule. The Lakewood Church, we discovered on our arrival, was born in the vision and dedication of the people of the First Evangelical Free Church of St. Paul, Minnesota. A few concerned individuals began to pray about it. Those prayers were not answered until November 1969 when Rev. Donald Leigh began to hold meetings in the Parkview School.

The decision to start a new work was not without opposition. Few objected openly until several families in prominent positions of leadership announced that they were going to join the new congregation. This crystalized the thinking of some who had been vaguely disturbed by the new project but had not expressed their fears.

They were concerned that the new group was siphoning off some of their leadership and financial support. However, First Church continued to prosper financially and spiritually. New leadership was raised up to fill the void dissenters thought would be left when the nucleus left to begin the White Bear Lake congregation.

Starting with 10 families in November 1969, the new church gained 20 new families the first year, 35 the second, and 73 in 1973. Attendance jumped from 27 the first month to a high of 300 in May 1974, and an average attendance of 275 during the summer months, when there is often a decline. There were 38 new members the last full year before our visit. All joined by confession of faith. In the same period of time there were 27 first-time decisions for Christ and 14 for consecration. Most of the latter two groups were adults.

"There was some duplication," Pastor Leigh informed us, "but at least half of the new members were brought to Christ earlier and a number of those who made decisions last year have not yet joined the church."

Bible studies began more than a year before the first Sunday meetings were launched, starting with an informal get-together in the home of Dr. Harold Broman on July 4, 1968. He and his family lived in North St. Paul where he was practicing medicine, and there were few truly evangelical witnesses in the area. There were other families with Free Church background living nearby who did what they could to help get the new church started.

Rev. Donald Leigh was involved in the ministry from the

beginning. He and his wife attended the prayer meetings and took part in the discussions concerning the structure and purposes of the local church.

"There was a new dimension we felt we should seek," he told us. "We were influenced to some extent by books on the subject of new concepts in church methods, but the guiding philosophy we went by was developed in our meetings.

"I will have to confess to having given birth to some of the ideas that went into our program. Some came from Dr. Don Larson, a faculty member at Bethel College. Some came from the people as we studied the scriptural accounts of the early church."

As the months passed, the outline of their goals and purposes came into focus. The church's evangelistic thrust, they decided, would have to be on a one-to-one basis, with the laymen actively involved.

"I could never do the work our people can do in reaching others for Christ," Leigh explained.

A prominent layman in the group went into more detail regarding their church philosophy. "I know it isn't original, but we see the duties of the pastor as being somewhat similar to those of a general directing and challenging his troops. He is more attuned to the needs of the people, spiritually, and its his responsibility to develop programs and methods to help meet those needs and present them to us for our consideration. We laymen run the church, but at the same time we don't feel our pastor is working for us. He works for Jesus Christ and is answerable to Him."

Biblically, they decided, every believer is to be a missionary. They know that God does not want everyone to go to a foreign field, or even to another part of the country. But he does want them to work for Him.

"We saw that He might want us to work in the hardest field of all," he continued. "He may want us to share Jesus Christ on the street and in the neighborhood where we live, or at the place where we work. There are people each of us can influence for Christ more effectively than anyone else. It's our job to seek out those people and share our Lord with them."

They were not opposed to door-to-door visitation, but didn't plan on doing any.

"There are so many sects pounding the streets these days," Leigh said, "that we have the feeling we would be 'turned off' before we got started."

It was their conviction that one's influence would be the greatest where he is the best known.

"This is one place where the adaptability of our group comes in," Dr. Broman said. "The accepted way of visitation is to have a night set aside for it and saturate a given area with workers."

"That's right," another layman broke in. "From past experience we have concluded that it is more effective for our people to visit and witness where they are known. So, even though it is easier the old way, we have been encouraged to conduct our church calls differently. Anybody can go across town where no one knows him and knock on doors. It's something else to talk to those you live and work with."

We were beginning to understand why Harold and Margaret Broman were so excited about their church and why he had spoken of the flexibility of their approach. If this was an indication of the way things were done, the church was adaptable to the needs of the people they were trying to reach.

According to the pastor the Bromans are the kind of people who take the principle of witnessing around home and at work seriously. We heard little from them about their own efforts to share Jesus Christ. Rev. Leigh related the story of one of Harold's patients, Margo, who appeared unannounced at the door of the doctor's home one morning.

"Are you Dr. Broman's wife?" she asked.

When Margaret assured her that she was, the visitor took half a step backwards and surveyed her critically, from her sweat shirt to her cut-off jeans and bare feet.

"I've got to find out what makes you tick. I've been doctoring with that husband of yours. He's so different from anyone else I know that I decided I just had to come over and see what his wife is like."

That was the beginning of a friendship that eventually was to bring an entire family to Jesus Christ. A year to the day after she became a believer, she prayed with her own mother who was living with them. Then her mother joined her in praying for her two brothers.

But the story does not end there.

The following Saturday, the day before Easter, Margo's husband, Mike, came to church to meet with the pastor.

"I don't know what it is that my wife's got," he said bluntly, "but whatever it is, I want it."

On Easter Sunday the entire family came to the Sunrise Service breakfast, Sunday school, morning worship and the evening service.

Mavis, a handicapped girl who weighs less than 100 pounds, also accepted Christ as a result of the witnessing of the doctor and his wife. They first got acquainted with her when she was a patient of Harold's. As a result of her testimony, that of Harold and Margaret, and a Men's Retreat at Camp Shaminaw, Mavis' 6'5" husband, Dave, also made a profession of faith.

A young Roman Catholic medical student who came to work with Harold was at a crisis point in his faith and chose to follow Christ and let Him have control of his life. (His fiancee was a believer.)

And so it has gone.

"When Harold and Margaret latch onto a couple, they'd just as well become believers right away," Rev. Leigh said. "They'll pray for them and keep working with them until they come through, regardless of how long it takes."

John and Jan Elmquist are good examples of the way the members of the little congregation work to reach their friends and neighbors. At the time we were in White Bear Lake there were five families in the church as the direct result of their witness.

And there are others who share Christ with the same care and devotion, many of them. The laymen of Lakewood Church are faithful in reaching out to others whose need is Jesus Christ.

By design the people make no effort to bring unchurched kids into the Sunday school. Unlike so many churches, they have no buses and no organized visitation. If kids come without their parents, the people see that they are made welcome and follow-up visitation may be done in the home if it appears that would be advisable, but no concerted attempt is made to get kids there.

"We lack the space to take care of them, for one thing," Rev. Leigh explained to us, "but our basic philosophy is definitely not aimed at reaching children. It's this way:

"If you reach the child, the influence of the home is such

that you must say in honesty, 'Maybe we have the child.' If you reach the mother, you have the mother and *maybe* you have the child. The father's influence is still so great he can undo everything else that has been done. But if you reach the father, you have, in most cases, reached the entire family for Jesus Christ."

So their efforts are family oriented with the primary emphasis on reaching the father.

"We have seen this pay off time after time," the pastor said. "The growth of our church is coming largely from new converts who are being reached, as families, by the Christian families in our congregation. That is one of the things that makes the church so exciting."

Few churches would even consider putting their youth pastor into the difficult position of guiding a new congregation through the long period of gestation and birth. Yet that is exactly what the St. Paul congregation did.

Rev. Donald Leigh, who received his college degree from Taylor University and his Master's from Gordon Divinity School, came to First Evangelical Free Church of St. Paul as associate pastor with youth his major responsibility. When the church finally reached the place where they were ready to organize a new work, they asked him to take on that responsibility.

A young man with a good education, tact and an understanding of people and the art of working with them, he has proven to be most effective. In talking of his leadership one of the men said that at first he didn't seem to be strong in that department.

"The pastor never gives the impression of trying to force something through in spite of what we think about it. But he is a man of ideas, is persuasive in presenting them, and when we decide on a course of action, he is able to choose exactly the right people to implement the program. He's really a terrific leader."

In 1970 the First Evangelical Free Church of St. Paul made a down payment on the land that had been chosen as the site for the new building. They also paid three-fourths of the pastor's salary to help the newly established Lakewood Church. In '71 and '72 their assistance was also substantial, but the fourth year it was cut back, by mutual agreement, to a few hundred dollars. The new church also had help from the denomination to the extent of $6,200 from the Shareholders' Fund, a short-term loan for $10,000 which was soon paid off, and a long-term loan for the same amount which is still outstanding.

When the people first started holding services in White Bear Lake, they rented the gym in a neighboring school. That was quite satisfactory for the winter and spring months, but as summer approached the custodian was disturbed. An ardent fisherman, he didn't like the idea of having to be at the school for both Sunday morning and evening.

He let the pastor and the board know that he didn't mind being on hand for the early Sunday service, but he wished they would find another meeting place for Sunday night. It was then that the congregation came up with the idea of meeting in the backyard of one of the homes for a potluck supper, a time of fellowship and devotions.

"I wouldn't be surprised if God gave us a fishing janitor to get us out of the school building on Sunday nights and into the homes," one of the men said. "It was a tremendous way for us to get acquainted and to learn to love each other."

"It was a way the Lord could help us all to get to know the newcomers who visited on Sunday nights, too," the pastor added. "It was summer time and everything about the meeting was informal so no one felt a particular need to dress up. We would have a couple of kids who played guitars accompany our singing, and I would give a ten-minute object lesson to illustrate a Bible truth. It was great."

With only the gymnasium for services before the church building was finished, they could not have Sunday school classes divided along traditional lines. There wasn't enough space. They developed a program to help them get the most out of the situation they were in. They had a main lesson for half the period, consisting of a film or a film-strip related to a Bible study. For the balance of the time they divided into six groups by handing out colored slips of paper at random each Sunday. Those with the same color paper went into the same class. It meant that a 75-year-old man might be in the same class with a 10-year-old. They would discuss the Bible lesson portrayed on the film.

One lad, who was six or seven, came up to the pastor after

they had been operating that way for several weeks.

"I don't understand what they're talking about most of the time," he said, "but I sure like it."

Earlier Rev. Leigh had seen one of the men standing with his arm about the boy's shoulder. The lad felt as though he was an individual the man knew and liked.

"I'm convinced that sort of acceptance by the adults will do more for the kids than a month of lessons geared for them," the pastor told us.

The experts would be properly horrified at seeing a Sunday school operated in such a haphazard manner, but those who were involved in it were well pleased with the results.

From the beginning they decided to have the Sunday worship service at 9:30 with coffee fellowship and Bible classes following. This resulted in nearly everyone staying for the Bible classes. The pastor had given the Sunday school teachers from junior high through the adult classes an outline of the morning sermon and a short commentary on it, to help them lead a profitable discussion on the message.

One father, who admitted to being cool to the idea at first, said he had changed his mind. "Now, on the way home from church, we discuss the message of the morning, and the Bible passages the pastor suggests for us to read each day throughout the week sort of reinforce what he said in his sermon."

"And the kids like it as much as we do," his wife put in. "They really listen during the worship service and the Sunday school discussion."

During the summer the fellowship suppers are carried out each Sunday night in the backyards of the various members of the congregation. They also have a similar dinner once a month at the church during the winter.

"The people say the fellowship is so wonderful they don't want to miss a single supper," the pastor explained.

The prayer meetings, like the Sunday night services that first summer, had to be held in different homes.

"Again God used circumstances to bring about a situation that could be a blessing to our little group," Rev. Leigh continued. "There were only four of us at the prayer meeting the night the turning point in prayer came at Lakewood."

The people who owned the home where they were meeting

weren't even there. They had gone on vacation and left the key with the Leighs so they could get in for the Wednesday night meeting.

The discussion that night was on group prayer and what they wanted for their church. They decided to ask God for ten new families by the end of the year. The minister was so moved by the way the Spirit seemed to be leading that he wrote down the day and the covenant they were making to pray daily for this goal for the church.

"By the end of the summer God had given us fifteen new families," Rev. Leigh told us, eyes still glowing at the marvelous way God had answered their prayers. "And it wasn't through my preaching. They came because of the witness of the individual members of our little group. After that the idea of praying specifically for a certain goal in the church spread to others in the congregation.

"We now pray for each other by name and for our loved ones and the unsaved friends we're burdened for. And we pray that God will direct us to just the right means of presenting Christ to our unbelieving friends and relatives. It's so important to witness to them in a way they will respond to."

As we saw the church it was adaptable to the needs of the people they were burdened for. Prayer was the secret of the success of that adaptability. The Holy Spirit had to guide or the best plans and efforts would be ineffective.

o   o   o

The Lakewood Church began with a Bible study, and such studies have had an important place in its ministry ever since. There are studies for women during the day, others for men, and still others for couples. There is even one Bible study that meets every Wednesday night in one of the homes in spite of the fact that it conflicts with prayer meeting.

"I had to do some serious soul-searching when I realized that Wednesday night was the only night of the week when some of those we have been concerned about reaching could meet for Bible study," the pastor said. "I like to have a large prayer meeting as well as any minister. I'm convinced that a church that prays will go forward. When this matter was brought to my attention I wasn't anxious to have the group meet as it would cut down on our prayer meeting attendance.

"But God convicted me of that. I realized that as a church we have to be flexible enough to change to meet the needs of our people. To stop that Bible study because of the conflict could very well mean we would lose our best opportunity to reach those unchurched who could attend on Wednesday night. So I went to the couples from our church who were involved and urged them to stay with the other group. Frankly, I *know* I made the decision God would have had me make."

The Horns are one of the church families who has a Bible study in their home. They, too, have seen encouraging results. They invited their friends, Tom and Judy, whose lives have been completely transformed.

Judy is one of a family of twelve and was greatly burdened for her brothers and sisters once she became a Christian. She witnessed to them and saw nine of the twelve receive Jesus Christ between the fall of 1973 when she and her husband were converted and the spring of 1974.

It was through Bible studies, at least one of which was the same study that meant much to the growth of Lakewood, that the change came about at St. Peter's Catholic Church in North St. Paul. Three of the women from Lakewood were involved in a major way in the study that included some Catholic women. There were a number of conversions among the Catholics as well as the others and the group continued to grow rapidly.

When it got so large they had to divide, a priest, who had recently given his heart to Christ, invited one group to meet in the parish house. They accepted his invitation but he refused to lead them, saying he didn't know enough about the Bible.

"So they invited Pastor Leigh to teach for six weeks and Pastor Ivar Blomberg, a Conservative Baptist minister serving a church in the area, also taught the class for the same length of time. Then the priest took over.

Margaret Esher, who is very active in St. Peter's, became a Christian, too, as a result of the Bible studies. (There are now several Bible studies operating solely within the membership of the church in addition to those which have Protestants in them.) Margaret helped prepare the bulletins and got permission to insert Bible readings for each day of the week.

"She didn't know what to suggest," Rev. Leigh told us, "so

she would call me every week for suggestions. I gave her the Bible readings I prepared for our church and she put them in their bulletins."

As we drove past St. Peter's that Sunday afternoon with Dr. Broman, he told us of the impact the gospel is making there.

"I'm not sure I know the full extent of it," he said, "but I do know there are many, many believers now who are dedicated completely to Jesus Christ."

Some Catholics left the church when they received Christ. Others have chosen to remain. Those who stay have no special problems, but those within the church who have not been touched by the gospel are completely bewildered by what they are seeing and hearing.

The 1973 budget of the Lakewood Church shows only $3,900 out of $47,000 going for missions. This meager sum is partially because most of the people who are coming into the church have no evangelical background and lack a burden for missions. They see the need of those who live across the street but not those across an ocean.

Part of the lack of interest in missions comes from the pastor's attitude, although he took the summer of 1974 away from the church and went to British Columbia where he and his family lived in an isolated Indian village to help a missionary. He told us that he sees sending Americans to other countries as missionaries (except in the case of specialists) as a waste. The work should be done by nationals.

On Sunday night as we were finishing our work at the Lakewood Church, Gordon Engdahl, a prominent member of the congregation, approached us. He was concerned about some areas of the church. He was excited about the things that were happening in the Bible studies but saw the possibility of problems developing.

"There are so many outsiders that there's a possibility the groups could become divisive and schismatic," he said.

He was also troubled about the financial base of the church.

"Seventy percent of the money we receive comes from twenty percent of the people," he continued. "That's understandable because so many of the new people are either from denominations where they have never learned to give or are from unchurched backgrounds. Stewardship has to be taught and that requires time."

Then there was the matter of the bonds they had sold in order to build the church. Out of $250,000 in bonds their own people bought $100,000. The balance were sold to relatives or concerned friends on the outside.

"You can see what a tremendous responsibility that places on our small membership," he concluded.

"I'm concerned about the things Gordon mentioned," Harold Broman acknowledged, "but I know he would agree with me that God has brought us this far, and if we are careful to seek His guidance in every detail, He will see us through."

We had a letter from a member of the congregation several months after our visit.

"We are now averaging 276 in our morning worship services even though our pastor is still in British Columbia for the summer. And souls are being saved. It's like a young man said in a time of sharing last Sunday, 'Just think, some of the newest believers in Christ have never even met our pastor. They came to the church for the first time since he's been away.' "

There was a prayer of thanksgiving in our hearts.

Digging into what had been happening at Lakewood Church and the reasons for it proved to us that adaptability was an important principle in an effective church. Although the programs of the Minnesota congregation and Fort Worth's Bible Church could not possibly have been farther apart if the pastors had deliberately set out with that as their goal, both churches are exploding according to our definition of the term. Each was successful because each is meeting the needs of the people they are attempting to reach.

Our list of principles for having a growing church increased by one.

1. ANALYSIS AND EVALUATION
2. STRONG BIBLE EMPHASIS
3. LOVE
4. ADAPTABILITY

12

The Neighborhood Church,
Castro Valley, California

When we went to Castro Valley to research the Redwood Chapel and the Neighborhood Church°, we intended to use only one. Strangely enough, we could not choose between them. Each in its own way was outstanding. We make no apology for writing up both churches, even though they are a scant two miles apart.

○ ○ ○

We have long believed that program is at the bottom of the list insofar as the principles behind exploding churches is concerned. A congregation must have a deep, abiding love for Christ, for fellow believers and those who are not Christians, and it must be adaptable to the needs of the people, getting down where they live. Only after all the other conditions are met is program important.

Dr. Jacob Bellig, senior pastor of the Neighborhood Church in Castro Valley, California, would be quick to agree with that appraisal. He finds it disturbing to have the church he serves known for its unusual program when other elements of the ministry are so much more important.

When we began our interviews at the Neighborhood Church, we soon discovered that every principle on our list was vividly

---

° Also known as the Cathedral at the Crossroads.

and effectively represented in the church. We could have ably justified placing this particular congregation in any category. Yet the outstanding program the senior pastor and his staff have put into effect kept crying out to us. Deliberately we refrained even from discussing it until our research was finished.

That was the situation when we dismissed our cab a few minutes before 11:30 in the morning and hurried up the broad stairs in the new building overlooking the freeway in Castro Valley. For the past several days we had been looking over their spacious facilities and gathering material from the members of the staff. Now we were to complete that phase of our work by interviewing senior pastor, Dr. Jacob M. Bellig.

A young Spanish-American couple was also waiting in his office to see him. They had approached a member of the staff about being married in the church and were referred to Dr. Bellig. He invited them in as graciously as though he had nothing else planned for the day.

The dark-haired young man was so nervous he neglected to close the door and we could not avoid hearing the conversation. They weren't members of the church. Actually, they had only visited a few times, but the building was so beautiful with those three towering crosses on the rim of the hill, that they had decided they would like to be married there.

Pastor Bellig checked the calendar and asked about the ceremony. He himself would like to officiate.

Then, subtly, the subject of the conversation changed. For the next 30 or 40 minutes he presented Christ to them. They made no decision as a result of that visit, but in those few minutes a bond had been forged between themselves and the church that could be the deciding factor in the direction their lives would eventually take. When they left he walked to the head of the stairs with them and gave them two booklets which they promised to read.

Bellig apologized for the delay.

"When church members or fellow believers come in to ask about being married in the church, one of the other men usually handles it. When a couple like this asks to use the church for their wedding, I have asked the men to refer them to me."

A few minutes later he said he hoped we would not look at this church as something that could only happen in California.

"We do have some *different* programs," he acknowledged. "I'm thinking particularly of our illustrated sermons. But we don't use them to entertain. This church is not in the entertainment business. They are the bait we use in fishing for the souls of men. No other type of service we've been able to come up with will consistently bring from 1300 to 1600 out on Sunday night, and with half of them completely outside the church of Jesus Christ."

He needn't have been concerned. We had already seen him and his church at work. We saw his love for the unbeliever in the kindly way he talked with the couple who had just left his office. We had seen that same love and burden for the lost evidenced in the members of the staff as we taped their accounts of how they were serving God through the Neighborhood Church.

With a church family of 3,000, a budget of $750,000, including $100,000 for missions and a Sunday school averaging more than 1700, the interdenominational Neighborhood Church presents a forceful witness for Christ.

According to Dr. Bellig, from 150 to 200 young people have gone out from the congregation into various avenues of Christian service. That figure speaks eloquently of the church's effective witness.

The illustrated sermons at Neighborhood Church bring non-Christians from all over the San Francisco area to visit on Sunday nights. Its Port O'Call for service men is known on every ship and in every Air Force squadron and every Army division around the world. Both programs have been the means of bringing hundreds to a saving knowledge of Jesus Christ.

The 'hot-line,' a program providing counseling and a sympathetic ear by telephone twenty-four hours a day, seven days a week, holds out hope and the hand of Christ to the lonely, the bewildered and the despairing.

"The important thing for every program we have is to reach people for Christ," Pastor Bellig went on. "It isn't the tools that mean so much. The secret lies in the fact that God uses His people to reach others for Christ. There is no shortage of sinners. There is only a shortage of witnesses and a lack of love and concern on the part of God's people.

"If the church succeeds, the minister can't take credit for that success. God must get the glory. On the other hand, if it fails, the minister has to take the blame. I've seen it proved repeatedly that if God's men prayerfully work with him in any situation, allowing Him to guide them, the church will eventually get going.

"Now I don't de-emphasize program to the point where I believe it's possible to tack any old idea together in the time it takes to give the commercials between TV programs and come up with something successful. The Scriptures tell us that what we do, we should do well.

"Motive lies at the heart of the matter. Do we want a big Sunday school so we can put a sign on the church boasting about it? Or are we trying to reach young lives for Christ?

"When we have done our very best for the right motive we can say, 'Lord, do what we can't do.' "

The Neighborhood Church was located in Oakland when Rev. Jacob Bellig was called to become its pastor. He was well acquainted with the illustrated sermons even before he was asked to take the church. The former pastor, Earl Sexauer, who originated them, had talked with him often about the program. It began very simply at first. Knowing the effectiveness of drama, he had people act out some of the Bible passages used in his evening messages. Members of the congregation caught the vision of the dramatized sermons as a means of outreach. When they built their new church, the nave was planned and constructed to accommodate their unique Sunday night services. The seating arrangement more closely resembled a theater than the traditional sanctuary, and the platform had hydraulic lifts under various sections so sets and scenes could be arranged in the basement and raised into place.

The illustrated sermons were well received and were reaching souls for Christ, but they did not enjoy universal acclaim from the Christian community. Actually they met a certain amount of open opposition and the scorn of many who considered them too theatrical.

Pastor Bellig was one of those who didn't buy the concept. He told his wife he would never preach an illustrated sermon. He shared his feelings with the board.

"The important thing is not the illustrated sermons," one of the men on the board spoke up with deep insight. "Or whether you will use them or not. I can't believe God cares one way or the other about that. The important thing is that we reach as many people as possible for Jesus Christ."

"God used those words to rebuke me, gently," the pastor related. "I tried the illustrated sermons in spite of my own misgivings and was encouraged by the results. During this transition time Rev. David VonRotz, who had worked as assistant pastor for five years with my friend, Earl Sexauer, was helping me in planning and staging my first illustrated sermons."

Von Rotz is an organist of professional quality and uses his talent at that instrument in the services and radio broadcasts. Today, he is an associate pastor who has held every position on the staff at one time or another in the more than twenty-six years he has been at the Neighborhood Church.

Dr. Bellig learned to enjoy this new (to him) method, and when they were planning their present building they again had the nave designed particularly for the Sunday night services. The seating arrangement is much the same as that in an opera house and there are two hydraulic stages to facilitate the changing of scenes. There is one full-time worker involved in the illustrated sermons, a professional artist who used to paint sets for the San Francisco Opera Company before his conversion. The hundreds and hundreds of costumes have all been sewn by members of the congregation. The spotlights are operated by volunteers, and other unpaid workers help the artist make changes in the scenes. The actors and actresses are drawn from those who are interested in the church.

"If we use dialogue," one of the staff members said, "we take it from the Living Bible or one of the other modern paraphrases or translations."

They will often call on the music department for background music and occasionally will use soloists, small groups, or the choir.

At times they will have 75 or 100 characters in a scene. Only Bible passages or themes are acted out. The entire sermon is never dramatized.

Although the popularity of the illustrated sermons increases along with their outreach and they continually draw people to the church, the board has never felt there were sufficient funds available to warrant going on television. However, two months before our visit a Christian man from outside the San

Francisco area got interested in helping get the program on television.

"Don't worry about money," he told Pastor Bellig when he learned the reason they were not being televised. "I'm interested in this work."

The plans had not been finalized at the time of our visit, but a preliminary format for two illustrated sermons was worked out. A patriotic sermon would be aired in the fall if the many details and problems could be worked out, and a Christmas sermon later on.

"I think we would do four a year to begin with," the minister told us. "Then we would increase it to eight if the interest and support warrants the increase. From there we would consider adding additional sermons as we could. We plan no huge drive for funds for television and do not anticipate making it a big thing."

Although the illustrated sermons attract such wide interest and are so spectacular they set the Neighborhood Church apart, Pastor Bellig feels they are far from being the most important area of the work.

"On the basis of my total experience in the ministry," he volunteered. "If I had to choose one tool above all others, I'd stick with the Sunday school. A church can get to the entire family with a Bible witness by going through the children you're able to get into the Sunday school."

Their Sunday school program is much like that of most good churches. It stresses a strong Bible orientation from the beginners through every adult class, effective, dedicated leadership in the office of the Sunday school superintendent and well-trained teachers. They also operate six buses, a meager fleet by some standards, but the church feels they have all they need.

"We go out to Fremont, thirty miles from here," Bellig said, "because some of our people live out that way. We get good bus drivers who are concerned about evangelism and place them in charge of their buses.

"We cooperate with every city-wide campaign that comes to this area if we can agree generally with the theology of the evangelist; however, I'm convinced that one of the most effective ways of reaching the lost is through the personal witness of godly laymen."

The pastor went on to say that witnessing has another result. If a man is busy for Jesus Christ he is less apt to have spiritual problems himself.

o   o   o

The church has the traditional Bible study and prayer meeting on Wednesday night. On Tuesday night a Bible study is held at Port O'Call, and on Thursday night the Bible Study Fellowship meets. But that is not all. There is a study for singles, others for the high school gang, the college and career groups, for couples, for men and for women. There are also Bible studies on Wednesday morning for those of both sexes who cannot get to an evening group.

o   o   o

"Any success we have seen at the Neighborhood Church," Dr. Jacob Bellig told us, "is due to the consecrated laymen and the dedicated, well-trained staff God has brought to us. The staff is responsible for the various departments of the church and the laymen help them make the programs go."

There is strong leadership from the senior pastor down through the staff to the laymen who help make the program a reality. Men and women with special talents and abilities work long hours in every department.

Ed Harris, a convert of Port O'Call, is now in charge of the junior high youth. There are 160 or more under his direction. It is his responsibility to present Jesus Christ to them, to help both old and new converts to reach spiritual maturity and to be concerned about those who have never trusted in Christ.

"It is definitely an outreach program," Harris told us. "Half of those kids will be in Sunday school but not in the morning service and many of them have no other contact with the church."

He talks with his teachers once a quarter, questioning them about their classes.

"My goal is that by the end of one year each teacher will

know the spiritual standing of each kid he teaches. In order to help them reach that goal I question them in detail once each quarter. 'Have there been any decisions for Christ in your group? Have you visited with them personally so you can make some kind of spiritual evaluation?' "

Harris told us about the daughter of one of the local professional men who started coming to some of the junior high activities. Her interest in Sunday school was kindled and before long she received Jesus Christ as her Saviour. Her brother was the next to make a decision, then her mother. Both became believers because of the witness of the girl.

One father started coming to the gym to see his sons play in the junior high basketball league. The boys both made decisions for Christ and it wasn't long until their dad began to attend services.

"He hasn't become a Christian yet," Harris said, "but his boys are praying for him."

A Chinese lad the same age also made a decision for Christ at about the same time. His mother was so impressed by the change that had come over him that she, too, became a believer.

"The junior high kids today are more afraid of what their peer group will think of them than they ever have been before. That can really put the pressure on. And they aren't as bold in voicing their faith, if they have any, as they will be when they get in high school and college."

Force A, the Advanced Leadership Training Program for the Junior High Department, came about because some of the youngsters didn't think the Sunday school lessons were advanced enough to challenge them.

"Do we *have* to study that Micky Mouse stuff all the time?" they asked Harris.

The kids had asked for something with a challenge and Harris did not disappoint them. He couldn't find any material he felt was suitable, so he wrote his own, a wide-ranging study embracing practical Christian living, church doctrine and the place of a vital church in today's troubled world. Other similar subjects were also covered. The effort was so effective it is now a part of the regular curriculum.

A more advanced program is conducted for the high school and college age groups. Associate pastor, Paul Travis, is in charge. "The groups meet once each week and the programs are designed to build up the concerned young person in his faith and to speak to him about full-time Christian service."

Anyone can come who will discipline himself to study and who seems to have some leadership qualifications. They force themselves through an intense study and take time to practice what they have learned. There were three young men in the Internship Program who made decisions to go into the ministry, at least partially the result of their training, in the period from the first of May to the end of 1973. And, according to Travis, there is another in full-time Christian service, who is the most exciting individual to have participated in the program thus far.

"He doesn't have any Bible training except the Bible study he attended at the church and a six months' period in the internship group, but he has conducted three or four crusades in other churches," Rev. Travis said. "Just one like him makes the entire project worthwhile."

Beach Head is a program with a slightly different emphasis. It is designed to make the rank and file Christian aware of ways to reach souls for Christ in the form of 'on the job training.'

"People are won for Christ," Rev. Travis told us, "but the kids who go out come to realize that the people out there are real and they're hurting. More important, they see that they can do something about it."

They are given a short period of instructions in the way to use the four spiritual laws booklet and are taken to the beach to witness. According to our source of information every person who has taken part in the program has had the joy of leading someone to Jesus Christ. On an average day at the beach approximately 25 are reached for God. They are all referred to a local church near their homes. The church is notified and is asked to follow through with them.

Paul Travis told of the change the experience made in his own daughter's personality. Shy and introverted, she was almost ill at the thought of approaching a stranger. She went timidly with a friend. An hour or so later she came running back to the bus.

" . . . I thought this was going to be hard, but it's easy. People didn't bite my head off."

Later she told her father that he was right when he said that shyness is sinful pride.

                              °   °   °

The Singles program has been a part of the Neighborhood Church ministry for a number of years, but it limped along until about a year before we went to Castro Valley. They held a summer retreat in 1973 with a young singer and his accompaniest from Kansas City furnishing the program.

"I'm not sure just why it happened," Jim Davis, the director of Public Relations, told us, "but that retreat was the match that kindled interest in our Singles program."

A second retreat was scheduled for September and the program took off. There were those who had never married, those who were divorced or separated from their mates, and those who were separated by death. Each group had its special problems, its special needs, but all were faced with certain basic problems—that of loneliness and the feeling of not belonging.

"Whether we want to admit it or not," Rev. Davis, who was in charge of the group, informed us, "our society is geared for couples. A good many singles feel as though they are second-class citizens."

A Bible study is a part of the program whenever they meet, but with one significant difference from what you would expect to find in an evangelical church. They always provide an alternative so those who come for the first time won't feel trapped.

"We don't want to give them the impression that we have the same attitude as a rescue mission—that they have to come in and sit through a Bible study or sermon in order to get a cup of coffee and a doughnut," we were told.

In spite of the fact that games are provided as an alternative, approximately half of those who come (90 to 100 from an average crowd of 200) take part in the hour-long Bible study. Following that there are a couple of hours of volley ball in the gym, and chess, checkers, password, monopoly or other similar games. It is not unusual for a large group to sit around, talking, until midnight or after. A number of Christians come to the meetings for the sole purpose of being available to counsel those who feel they have a special need or difficulty.

There are always unbelievers at each weekly meeting. Some are there because they have nothing else to do. Some think it would be a good place to meet someone they could date. Others are sent there by their friends, occasionally as a practical joke.

"If you want to get in on a real 'swingin' time, go out to the Neighborhood Church to their singles group," he may be told.

"We're glad for the publicity," one of the staff said. "It gives us a chance to present Christ to someone who probably never had a chance to hear about Him before."

An average of two people make decisions for Jesus Christ every week as a result of the singles ministry. Those are the figures that can be documented. In addition it is performing the purposes for which it was originally organized.

"It's made me feel as though I am important," one woman said, "even though I am not married. It has also made me realize that I can be of service in the church."

One woman in her twenties came to the group after she and her husband were separated. There were so many serious problems that divorce seemed to be the only answer. It wasn't long until she gave her heart to Christ and began to pray for her husband. After a few weeks he began to attend. Now he is a believer and they are back together again.

Another couple that was having real trouble and had also separated began to attend the singles meetings. They not only were brought back together but such a change had come into their lives and their marriage that they were asked to testify at one of the church meetings.

o   o   o

Back in 1964 Fred Ruhl and his wife were facing a difficult decision. Missionaries to China for three years and the Philippines for sixteen, they didn't know whether God would have them return to the field for another term or seek a ministry in the States.

"Then we got a chance to come here to the Neighborhood Church and be Chaplain at the Port O'Call," he told us. "It's been the greatest thing that ever happened to my wife and me. I would never have believed it possible that God would put us into a field so ripe with souls and so rich in harvest."

Port O'Call got its start in the heart of Mrs. Norene Bennet during the early days of World War II. She saw the young sailors flock to the San Francisco area and was so burdened for them she felt she had to do something. Enlisting the aid of several friends, she opened a small Servicemen's Center designed to reach them for Christ.

After a time God guided her to place the work under the umbrella of the Neighborhood Church. The leadership, facilities, and financial backing the church was able to provide helped the center to reach every goal she ever set for it, and more. Today the influence of Port O'Call stretches into every ocean and wherever the United States has military men. In fact, its influence goes farther. Men and women who have been reached for Christ through the center live in every state of the Union and many parts of the world. More have gone into full-time Christian service than anyone, anywhere has record of.

"I guess you could say I'm a Port O'Call baby," Rev. Ronald Story, now the pastor in charge of the high school youth, told us. "My folks met at Port O'Call. Dad was in service and Mom was a hostess. This church has been the center of our lives. Now I'm back here serving the Lord."

The program at the Port is almost as heavy as the one at the church, with the weekend load the heaviest. Servicemen with three days' leave flock to Port O'Call. It costs them nothing to stay there, they get good meals, and have access to a gym and pleasant surroundings.

"The Christian in uniform can't wait to get back to the Port once he's spent a weekend here," Mr. Ruhl told us.

But the ministry is not alone for the believer. Eighty-five percent of the men who use the facilities the church offers to servicemen are not Christians.

There are Bible studies and occasional activity during the week, but the place is comparatively quiet from Monday through Thursday. It comes alive over the weekend when passes are given out and the men pour off their ships and away from their camps. Teams of believers go to the bar-lined streets of San Francisco where the sailors and soldiers hang out and invite them to come to the Port.

The Friday night program is semi-social, with some sort of special event planned. The last Friday night of the month they have a birthday party for those who have had birthdays during the month. They all get a gift and have a great time.

"It won't take the place of a birthday at home," the chaplain said, "but it helps."

It is surprising how many of the boys enjoy visiting with Mom and Pop Ruhl, as they call them.

"I think chewing the fat with us reminds them a bit of home," the chaplain explained. "Most of the kids would never admit to being homesick, but they are—especially the younger ones who may never have been taken away from home for any extended time before."

Every Saturday night there is a party with hostesses who live in the area. (The hostesses are present other nights of the week, as well, but there are more on weekends.)

Not all the girls are believers but they are carefully screened. They all have high moral standards. Many of them come to the Port as a hostess and end up receiving Christ. It has become one more avenue of outreach, and quite unexpected by those who set up the program.

They decided on bringing in hostesses to help attract the boys and to give them a normal relationship with girls of character. The rules governing hostesses are rigid and some could be considered a bit laughable, but the guys expect them and the girls appreciate them. They know the regulations have been set up to protect them.

"If the rules are disregarded we warn them once or twice," Ruhl continued, "and if they don't shape up they can ship out. We seldom have to make a guy leave. They don't want to give up the privilege of enjoying the clean, wholesome atmosphere we provide. And besides, most of them recognize a clean, decent girl and respect her too much to make passes at her.

"We have five sets of games, each indicated by a day. There are some we play on Tuesday, others on Wednesday, and so on.

"Each guy has a different hostess for each game so he can't monopolize a certain girl. The get-acquainted party concludes with a testimony meeting, a sing and a short evangelistic message, followed by a 'Billy Graham' type invitation to accept Christ. After the service we announce they are to find their Monday night date and take her out to dinner. Our cooks try to make the meal as different from assembly line chow as possible. The guys seem to appreciate the style with which the food is served as much as the meal itself. It is financed by the church."

Sunday is more regimented. It has to be. Breakfast is served at nine, church is at ten, and Sunday school is held for them back at the Port at eleven. Another home-cooked meal and they are free to play softball or have some other activity in the afternoon. They have supper at 5:00 and their own program at 5:45. In the evening they go to church. When it is over they return to the Port for COD ("Closing Off the Day with Jesus), an informal type of meeting where they express themselves. They share testimonies, sing and have prayer requests, followed by refreshments.

In addition to the times of fun and games, there are Bible studies practically every night of the week. The types of study varies from one night to the next and from year to year, but through all of them there is a strong thread of salvation.

The Port O'Call will average 200 to 250 during a normal week. For a number of years there have been an average of 400 to 500 converts each year. There is a strong follow-up program for those who profess Christ.

"I guess there are two things that work together in this area," Mr. Ruhl explained. "Pastor Bellig insists on a well-planned follow-up program for all who make decisions through the efforts of some phase of the Neighborhood Church ministry, and that includes the Port O'Call. Then there's my background as a missionary.

"We learned during our years in the Orient that it is necessary to ground the new convert deeply in the Word or the chances were that we would never completely remove him from Oriental paganism. Most of these kids are pagan, too, and have to be dealt with just as carefully and with as much love and consideration."

The staff takes the new believers through a Moody Press book entitled *Abundant Life*. They study one chapter a week for twelve weeks. When that three months' period is over, they are urged to go into a special training class.

"We don't leave them dangling," the chaplain announced firmly.

One fellow who first started coming to the Port several years ago was a real rebel. "I called him St. Louis," Mr. Ruhl told us, "because he was a fan of the St. Louis Cardinals and wore one of their baseball caps with his full uniform. I'd watch him swagger around, as big as a moose and twice as noisy, and I'd say, 'Lord, why can't you just send us average guys?'"

Then on a Tuesday night they split into small groups to study, and the chaplain left them that way during the time of prayer. It was a custom for them to pray around the circle. St. Louis looked up at Mr. Ruhl, totally astonished. When it came his turn he gulped hard and began.

"God, I never did this before, but here goes . . ." He prayed a couple of sentences and stopped to look up. "What do I say now, Pop?" he asked the chaplain.

He suggested a couple of words and St. Louis would pray again.

"That boy changed so drastically that you never would have known him," Ruhl concluded. "His parents were thrilled by what happened to him. They even drove all the way from St. Louis to Castro Valley so they could see the place where the miracle had taken place."

Ed Harris, the Minister of Junior High Youth at the church, is a product of the Port. He started coming there while he was stationed in the San Francisco area, received Jesus Christ as his Saviour, fell in love with one of the hostesses and married her, and now is back on the staff.

There is no way of knowing how many young men who made their decision to take Christ as their Saviour at the Port have gone on into God's work somewhere in the world, but their number is legion.

Mr. Ruhl has a special training class for those who are interested in working in a Christian Service Center. It has been going on for two years and one couple is already in the Los Angeles area directing the youth ministry of a church. Another couple moved to another section of California to start a Servicemen's Center there.

Through the Port O'Call, as with illustrated sermons, the

music program, Sunday school and visitation, the Neighborhood Church continues to reach farther and farther out in its efforts to touch lives with the love of Jesus Christ. And the results one sees are but the tip of the iceburg, while most lay hidden from sight.

Rev. David VonRotz, veteran staff member, dramatically declares that all the glory, growth and development of this living organism, which is Neighborhood Church, belongs to God. As far as organized religious bodies, Neighborhood Church is not the largest, but its capacity to believe God for a harvest of souls and enlarged borders (both in buildings and ministries) is unsurpassed.

When we concluded work at the Neighborhood Church the task was finished.

1. ANALYSIS AND EVALUATION
2. STRONG BIBLE EMPHASIS
3. LOVE
4. DYNAMIC LEADERSHIP
5. ADAPTABILITY
6. PROGRAM

13
Revitalize Your Church

The principles we discovered that make for a growing church may seem too simple to be effective. They are simple. Yet they were developed only after corresponding with more than 100 congregations and personally visiting at least 40. We worked a year on the project and travelled more than 30,000 miles across the United States and Canada.

In addition to the accounts you have read in these pages, each principle is proved by many, many other interviews with pastors and dedicated laymen all across the country. Our tape transcripts fill two file drawers and our research books a shelf in our library.

We are not suggesting that anyone bodily lift the methods of one church and transplant them. They may or may not be successful in another situation. Our search was for principles, the underlying philosophy upon which effective, growing congregations are built. You may find some of the methods described in these pages helpful. More likely, they will provide a springboard, a goad to your own creative abilities, causing you to develop methods particularly suited to your own people.

Although the methods described here may or may not be usable in another situation, these principles are valid. We *know* they will work anywhere. We have seen their success in huge city churches with large staffs and multiple services each Sunday. We have also seen them revitalizing smaller congregations all across the United States and Canada. They have worked for others. They will work in your church, regardless of its size or spiritual condition. They will change your congregation completely, bringing them closer to Jesus Christ and multiply their effectiveness in reaching out to others.

You must begin with the obvious.

ANALYZE AND EVALUATE

Go over everything that is being done in each department of the church.

"You can't assume anything at this point," Rev. Sherman Williams, senior pastor of Castro Valley's Redwood Chapel, said. "When I first talked with our board about doing this very thing, many of them thought it to be a waste of time. They were particularly defensive about certain departments, like the Sunday school. When they completed the survey and evaluated it, they learned that the very departments they thought were the best were the most ineffective."

Rev. Dale Warkentin of the First Mennonite Brethren Church in Wichita was also astonished at what such a project uncovered. "If I hadn't seen the results myself, I'm not sure I would have believed them."

(Warkentin used a computer for the raw material brought in by the questionaires in the PERT Evaluation Program so the people could be sure he would not learn their identity by their handwriting, but it is not necessary to have access to a computer for that purpose. The anonymity of the answers can be achieved in other ways.)

If you have the leadership ability of a Dr. Criswell or a Jack Hyles, you probably will not need outside help to learn what is actually being done in your church. Most pastors, however, lack the personnel and time to conduct an accurate analysis on their own. For them, the adaptation of the PERT Analysis (EVALUATION REVIEW TECHNIQUE, prepared by MARC, 919 W. Huntington Drive, Monrovia, California 91016) and the CHURCH GROWTH AND EVALUATION studies by Dr. Virgil Gerber (William Carey Library, Fuller Theological Seminary, California) will be particularly helpful.

STRONG BIBLE EMPHASIS

It has been our experience that most evangelical pastors and laymen feel that, regardless of other shortcomings, their church can be credited with a strong Bible emphasis. This is undoubtedly true insofar as the doctrine of salvation and the emphasis on the Bible as the infallible word of God is concerned. We learned, however, that many churches that would qualify as being fundamental are not teaching the Word to their people as effectively as they could.

Rev. Kenneth Lawrence, pastor of the Johnston Heights Free Church, told us he could see now that his earlier preaching had not been as helpful to the people he served as it could have been. "I still preach on subjects that are profound, doctrinally. I happen to believe that is one of my obligations as a pastor. I used to stop there, but I don't anymore. I make the explanation simple enough for a child to understand and always present a practical application to the spiritual truth I'm bringing. Now I always try to leave our people with something that will actually be of help to them. I'm sure this has been a factor in the growth of our church."

Dr. Leslie Madison, pastor of the Northwest Bible Church in Fort Worth, underscored Lawrence's conviction that the Bible must be presented simply. "You should see the simplicity of the Bible course we are using as an outreach. My first impression was that a ten-year-old kid would have been bored with it. But we soon discovered it was on the right level for the average individual outside the church. We've had wonderful results with those studies."

Pastor Dale Warkentin found the same thing to be true. "In fact," he said, "I believe most churches have the same problem we had. Their people probably don't know any more about the Bible than some of those who were coming to our church at the time of the survey. The only difference is that the pastors and concerned laymen may not be aware of it."

We learned something of the effectiveness of a simple presentation of the Word of God in the story of Mildred Chapel, a small congregation in the north woods of Minnesota. They have never had more than 100 in attendance on a given Sunday. Few of those who worship there have more than high school diplomas, and there has usually been a problem of raising enough money to pay the bills. Yet more than a score of outstanding full-time Christian workers, including Dr. George Christian Weiss, Missionary Director at Back to the Bible Broadcast, have come from that little group. Missionaries and pastors who were raised in that little church circle the globe.

The reason?

We asked that question of Arthur Weins, Director of the Italian field for the Gospel Missionary Union, whose father, Weins, was the pastor at Mildred Chapel during the period when many of the more outstanding Christian leaders from that area were children and young people.

"I've often wondered," he said. "Dad's ministry was quiet and straightforward. He emphasized the Bible. I guess that is the key."

"There was a love for the Word instilled in us that has stayed with us all through the years," Dr. Weiss told us in his office at Back to the Bible.

So, it is not enough to center the ministry of a church on the Word of God. The presentation must be simple and practical. The congregation must be able to understand the Scriptures if they are to effectively change lives.

LOVE

This is another principle that many believe is more present in the lives of their people than an interested outsider would observe. As we discovered in considering the principle of a strong Bible emphasis, LOVE must be a cornerstone of any church that would be truly effective.

Love shows itself in many almost unexpected places. We knew the small Baptist Church in Aitkin, Minnesota, to be warm and friendly when we attended there summers a number of years ago. Not until Jeri Heinneman was killed in a car accident, though, did we see the true depth of the love the people had for each other. Jeri was the only son of widow Sally Heinneman, who was very active in the church. At the time of his death certain members of the congregation were away on vacation, but the church board phoned until they located them. Vacations were cut short and those people came back to be with Sally.

"When one of us is hurt I guess we all suffer," Pastor Ivor Blomberg told us.

We saw that same love showing in the First Free Methodist Church in Seattle, Washington, in their monthly Sunday night Healing Hurting Hearts program.

"We started it a number of years ago when we realized that many, many people carry deep, bewildering hurts," Dr. Robert Fine said. "Those with problems are urged to come to that service so we can pray for them."

Some are youngsters who are afraid of the dark or are concerned about a test. Adults will ask prayer for their children or for themselves. Often someone is facing serious surgery or is suffering the agony of loneliness and grief after the death of a loved one. Occasionally someone asks prayer for healing, but usually the requests are for different types of problems.

"Our Healing Hurting Hearts program has had a greater effect on our people than we anticipated," the pastor went on. "We have discovered that we love each other deeply and are concerned about each other and our problems. Aside from the help given to individuals with their problems, this program has helped to make a 'family' of our congregation."

The Third Christian Reformed Church of Denver is another congregation with a strong emphasis on LOVE. A number of years ago members of the congregation began to go into the Latin-American section of Denver just off the business district to witness and hold services. As a result of that witness Sun Valley Chapel was organized and a missionary brought in.

"The missionary is paid the same salary as our own pastor," one of the people said. "Both men have given their lives to God's service. How could we justify two different salaries to our Lord?"

When new maps are bought for the Sunday school in the mother church, a check is made to see if new maps are needed at Sun Valley. If a new piano is bought for Third Church, a new piano is bought for Sun Valley if it is needed.

We saw LOVE in the churches of Canada that were touched by the revival of 1971-1972. The love for Christ broke down barriers between members of families, healing old wounds and uniting brother to brother, husband to wife, and mother to child.

In some ways LOVE is more difficult to program into a church than a STRONG BIBLE EMPHASIS. Given a pastor who believes and knows the Word, it is possible to work out a program that will include a strong Bible emphasis.

Love, however, cannot be willed by an act of the mind. It must come from the Holy Spirit as we allow Him to fill us with himself. Usually love is demonstrated one act at a time. In the Canadian revival it started with the pastor and the officers and leaders of the church. Beginning with confession where that was necessary, God's people got right with each other, with those outside the church and with God himself. A chain reaction set in—love begetting love until entire churches were transformed.

While love cannot be willed, the proper climate for love can be set up by the pastor and church leaders. Love will soon sprout and flourish.

LEADERSHIP

Too often we think of leadership as the unilateral actions of one strong-minded individual who has the rhetoric and singleness of purpose to push his program past the church board. While there are many such men in the ministry, there are other types of leadership, not as spectacular, perhaps, but just as effective.

"No," one layman told us, "our pastor isn't a strong leader. I don't think you could call him a leader at all."

Later in the interview he came back to the subject.

"I've been thinking about our pastor and his leadership abilities. He doesn't force his own way, but he is a man of vision. He knows what he wants to do and is close enough to the problems and strengths of our people to sense our needs. He will quietly present changes or additions to our program. If there is objection, he will back off, rethink his position and approach us again. When there is enough support for a given project, it is brought to the people and passed. He already has selected just the right individuals to get the new effort off the ground. Now that I think about it, he's a tremendous leader."

Dr. Jacob Bellig, pastor of the Neighborhood Church in Castro Valley, California, is just that kind of leader. Bellig selects his staff with care and encourages them to think creatively about their own departments.

"He goes quietly about the job of helping us to be more effective in our own areas of responsibility," one of his staff members told us. "He's a great leader. He maintains a low profile but each of us has the benefit of his experience and vision without having our own initiative stifled."

Few pastors could decide they want to be leaders like Dr. W. A. Criswell or Dr. Lee Roberson. Such men are born leaders. The skills and personalities necessary cannot be willed into being. However, most of us could do as Rev. Aaron Jaeger, pastor of the Crystal Lake Evangelical Free Church in Crystal Lake, Illinois, has done.

"I knew I was weak in the area of administration," he said, "so I began to study secular books on management. I learned how to select people for certain responsibilities and how to delegate authority. I used to be one of those guys who had to run everything. I tried to make every decision for every group in the church. And I had my share of problems because of it. Now we've got more harmony than I've ever had in a church I've served, and things are going forward better than ever. There may not be any connection between the two, but I'm convinced there is."

In short, Jaeger *learned* to be a leader. Any pastor who lacks such skills can do the same. If you would have an exploding church, it is imperative that you become a leader.

ADAPTABILITY

Hillside Church in Armonk, New York, had a number of Neighborhood Bible Studies which were leading women in the area to Christ. The pastor could have ignored them in his efforts to reach men in the area and bring them into the church, or he could have resigned himself to the fact that his church would have a largely female congregation. Instead, he adapted himself and the church program to the situation, using the women to bring men into the church. He instructed the counsellors in how to work with the new converts in applying the teaching of Christ to their daily lives. They were challenged with the opportunities they had of living Christ before their husbands and families so effectively they, too, would want to have Jesus Christ in charge of their lives. It worked.

Today Hillside has as many men in the congregation as the average church their size. Because they were adaptable to the needs of their people, they have been able to turn an apparant problem into an asset.

Covenant-First Presbyterian Church in Cincinnati has had a similar experience. The downtown church has an illustrious past dating back to 1790 when their first sanctuary was built. Dr. G. Campbell Morgan, whose books are still being studied, was one of the former pastors. So was Lyman Beecher, Harriet Beecher Stowe's father.

But the church fell on difficult times. Former members used to live within walking distance of the church, and there were plenty of others in the immediate neighborhood to afford an opportunity for outreach and growth. Then change came to the city. Expressways wiped out dozens of city blocks. Dozens of others were leveled by urban renewal projects designed to give the inner city a new face. Attendance and membership dropped off as families moved away. It looked as though the dry rot that was affecting most inner city churches was setting in and that the strength of the congregation would eventually be nibbled away.

Then in 1968 Rev. Harold Russell came to pastor the church. Traditionally the church had brief services every day during Holy Week, which were attended by no more than two dozen people. Building on that service they started a luncheon meeting on Ash Wednesday in 1969, which was five times as large as the crowd during Holy Week.

The meeting was so successful it was continued every week through May, when it was suspended for the summer. In October the luncheon meetings were started again. The crowd has increased until Ash Wednesday, 1974, there were 483 in attendance and the Lenten crowd averaged 400. New friends have been made for the church, souls are saved, and the membership is climbing steadily.

Ridgeview Hills Christian Reformed Church in Littleton, Colorado, could not be more different than the Presbyterian Church in Cincinnati. It was organized late in November, 1969, and John Hofman, Jr., the present pastor, came in 1972. There are a number of churches in the Littleton area, each attracting a certain number of followers.

"But it seemed to us that all too often there was a tendency on the part of the pastor and the board to hold themselves apart from the community," Pastor Hofman said. "We wanted people to feel that we were in the community to serve and that we cared about them. So, it was decided that we would make our building available to community groups whose use of the building would not violate our Christian principles."

The Optimist Club, Scouts, Recovery Group, and organization of concerned Christians working with junior high kids, and many others use their building. The carpets are soiled and a number of windows have had to be replaced in the Educational Unit, but the community response has been excellent.

"If it ended there," the pastor said, "I would feel we had failed in our purpose for opening our building, but it hasn't. We've made some excellent contacts with families who first began to come to our building to attend some other type of meeting, but now are seriously interested in the church. We've gained a large number of visitors and the number is increasing, and we've had families confess Christ and join the church because of the use our building is put to."

By being adaptable to the needs of the people in the community, the church is able to reach out to them with the gospel of Christ.

PROGRAM

In the period from 1961 to 1966 the Dauphin Way Baptist Church of Mobile, Alabama, was losing members. In that period, they dropped a third in attendance in both Sunday school and church. The closing of an army base in 1964 acclereated the decline. In 1967 Dr. Myron Webber became the pastor. One of his first acts was to appoint a long-range planning committee to see what they should be doing to better serve their people.

His approach was very similar to that of Rev. Sherman Williams, whose experiences at the Redwood Chapel in Castro Valley, California, were told earlier in these pages. Williams guided his board into a survey of each activity of the church. His goal was a Total Church Program. Or, as Dr. W. A. Criswell put it, "It's imperative that we have something for everyone at First Baptist (Dallas)."

Webber was looking for weak areas or omissions in the church program. As a result of that survey the 5,000-member congregation accepted the fact that they were a downtown ministry and launched a 20-year expansion program at a total cost of five million dollars. The Christian Life Center, a recreational activity building was put up first. Then a nursing home for those who needed full-time nursing care. Next they erected a retirement home. The fourth new building was an apartment building for young working women which provides a wholesome Christian atmosphere close to the church. The last building is to be a new worship sanctuary.

It did not stop there, however. They launched a clothing ministry for the needy that soon branched into furniture. "We are careful about passing out such items," business administrator James Neyland told us. "Usually they go to someone who has had a fire and has lost everything or, like a Cuban family we helped recently. When they came to Mobile they had absolutely nothing."

In April of 1970 they bought a number of buses and began to operate them in an area that was not being reached by anyone else. So many kids were brought in that they ran out of space and bought the property of a nearby private school so they could continue to expand their bus ministry.

A Day Care Center was established with more than 200 kids, and they have also started a Single Adults program. At the same time purely social activities and banquets have been trimmed drastically.

"Our concern is that every activity of the church has as its purpose advancing the Kingdom of Christ," Mr. Neyland went on. "Those programs of lesser value are pushed aside."

The average Sunday school enrollment has doubled and the average church attendance has almost doubled. In 1972 Dauphin Way led the Southern Baptist churches in the state with 426 baptisms.

Every principle in our list is evident in this vital, growing church.

Those principles have been effective in churches in British Columbia and California and Alabama. They have transformed both large and small congregations everywhere. They will work for you.

The steps are simple. Analyze the work being done in every division of your church and evaluate its success or lack of it, using the other five principles as your guide. Then begin to change and improve the problem areas. You will be thrilled as your church comes alive!

Bibliography

Briscoe, Stuart. *Where Was the Church When the Youth Exploded?* Zondervan Publishing House.

Chandler, E. Russell. *The Kennedy Explosion.* David C. Cook.

Criswell, W. A. *The Bible for Today's World.* Zondervan Publishing House.

Decision Magazine Staff. *Great Churches of Today.* World Wide Publications.

Engstrom, W. A. *Multi Media in the Church.* John Knox Press.

Fickett, Dr. Harold L., Jr. *Hope for Your Church.* Regal.

Gentry, Gardiner. *Bus Them In.* Church Growth Publications.

Green, Hollis L. *Why Churches Die.* Bethany Fellowship, Inc.

Hubbard, David Allan. *The Church, Who Needs It?* Regal.

Hill, Samuel S., Jr. *Southern Churches in Crises.* Holt, Rhinehart & Winston.

Keith, Billy. *Criswell, W. A.: The Authorized Biography.* Fleming H. Revell.

Kennedy, Dr. James. *Exploding Evangelism.* Tyndale House.

Mains, David R. *Full Circle.* Word.

McBeth, Leon. *The First Baptist Church of Dallas.* Zondervan Publishing House.

McQuilken, J. Robertson. *Measuring the Church Growth Movement.* Moody Press.

Monroe & Taegel. *The Witnessing Laymen Make Living Churches.* Words.

Murch, James DeForest. *The Protestant Revolt.* Crestwood Books

Olsen, Charles W. *The Base Church.* Forum.

Christian Life Magazine. "100 largest Sunday Schools." October, 1973 and October, 1974.

Palmer, Bernard. *Program for a Total Church.* Victor Press.

Palmer, Donald. *Explosion of People Evangelism.* Moody Press.

Richards, Lawrence O. *A New Face for the Church.* Zondervan Publishing House.

Roberson, Lee. *The Highland Park Baptist Church*. Highland Park Baptist Church.

Shedd, Charlie W. *The Exciting Church Where People Really Pray*. Word.

Tarr, L. K. *This Dominion His Dominion*. Fellowship of Evangelical Baptist Churches of Canada.

Towns, Elmer L. *America's Fastest Growing Churches*. Impact Books.

———.*America's 10 Largest Sunday Schools*. Impact Books.

———. *Great Soul-Winning Churches*. Sword of the Lord.

Cɘl

GENERAL BOOKBINDING CO.
79 4 A
137NY2 340 6036
QUALITY CONTROL MARK